BEAR CAVE HILL

BEAR CAVE HILL

(A MEMOIR)

JAMES M. SKIBO

iUniverse, Inc.
New York Lincoln Shanghai

Bear Cave Hill
(A Memoir)

Copyright © 2006, 2007 by James M. Skibo

iUniverse books may be ordered through booksellers or by contacting:

iUniverse
2021 Pine Lake Road, Suite 100
Lincoln, NE 68512
www.iuniverse.com
1-800-Authors (1-800-288-4677)

ISBN-13: 978-0-595-37939-2 (pbk)
ISBN-13: 978-0-595-82309-3 (ebk)
ISBN-10: 0-595-37939-7 (pbk)
ISBN-10: 0-595-82309-2 (ebk)

Printed in the United States of America

Acknowledgments

The events in this story are true to the best of my memory and all the people are real, though some names have been changed. I have many people to thank and it starts with my family. It is both a blessing and a curse to have a family member write a story of our shared path. I thank them all for their love and support and to jog my memory, when needed, of events from our past lives. My wife, Becky, is ever supportive even when projects like these sometimes take me far away. She also read the draft many times and provided useful comments. Our children, Matt and Sadie, also read the manuscript and provided helpful suggestions and their permission to make them part of the story. My mother (Rose Mae) and sisters (Mary Fran and Karen) provided useful comments and especially encouragement all along the way. Many friends read drafts of the manuscript or provided assistance. I am grateful to them for helping to make the book better and, most importantly, for convincing me that this was a story worth telling. They include Brett Arsenault, Gina Bessa, Bob Bjork, Marc Bjork, Rob Bligh, Lyman (deceased) and June Diercks, Eric Drake, John Franzen, Jeff Grathwohl, Kent Gursuch, Christine Holappa, Bill Longacre, Dave Malone, Bob Mangialardi, Joe Mikulecky, Norm Robertson, Dave Ruszkowski, Michael Schiffer, Dan Seger, Kasia Stadnik, Jim Stanlaw, and Christine Szuter. I would also like to thank Dawn Marano for her wise editorial advice that sent this book in a new and better direction. Finally, this story would not have been possible without my father, and I dedicate this book to his loving memory.

Contents

Chapter 1

Sled War

I always thought dad would live to 100 years old. He came up 17 years short. Twenty or so old soldiers passed by my dad's coffin, each stopping and snapping off a surprisingly crisp salute. I knew many of them: the retired undertaker, my high school math teacher, the guy who worked for the telephone company. Although we were in church, they still wore those familiar hats, which I had seen them wear many times in the Memorial Day or VJ-Day (Victory over Japan Day) parade. Most of the local veterans served, like my father, during WWII, but each week it seemed the local vets marched to another funeral to say farewell. Five of the old soldiers were part of the local color guard, and they looked smart in their uniforms. Just a month earlier my father traced these same steps as a member of the color guard, but today they would be marching without one of their own. At least half of the men in the line were slightly bent over or hobbled by an arthritic knee or a recent hip replacement, but as they approached my father's resting body they found their steel, straightened their backs, picked up their gait and readied for yet another soldier's final tribute.

Most of these men had known my father, some for the entire eight decades of his life, yet any emotion that they may have felt as they approached his coffin was covered over with so many years of old varnish that I didn't notice a single lip quiver. Fifty years after many of them had seen active duty they did the military proud. This stoic lack of emotion was a part of these men just as trees, rivers, and long tough winters are a part of the Upper Peninsula (U.P.) of Michigan. My Aunty Wanda used to say that people who grew up in the U.P., and especially descendants of the early 20th century immigrants, didn't complain much because if they ever started they would never stop. The only time you heard people from my home town talk about their feelings was when they said something like, "It

1

feels like rain." I am far removed from this place today. I am an archeologist and university professor in Illinois, but stoicism is still part of me, good or bad. I was getting a cup of coffee recently and some spilled on my hand making my colleague, standing next to me, grimace in pain. Somewhere inside I may have screamed, but it was buried so deeply within that I wouldn't have given it a second thought if I hadn't seen the look of alarm on her face. Like my father and his father before him, I had learned to take pain without emotion. But on the day of my father's funeral I was no doubt disappointing my ancestors as tears rolled down my cheeks as the old comrades paid their final tribute.

My wife's hand rested in mine as tears streamed down her face. I had called Becky at 5:00 a.m. several days earlier to tell her dad had died. I sat in my parents den and as we talked I looked at the gallery of pictures on the wall: weddings, grandchildren, and his smiling face. After choking off the story of dad's final hours, I just sat on the sofa and listened to Becky cry. I didn't say anything, just listened to her weep sadly. If you are not much of a crier it is probably important to have someone in your life who is. She wasn't doing it just for me, she loved my dad and he loved her, the way only a father can love the woman who loves his son. I also think he approved of the way she attacked life and worked hard. No greater compliment could come from my father than to say, he or she is a hard worker. She can roll up her sleeves and tackle a job as well as any of the Polish *babushkas* in my life. In this way, my wife is a good Polish woman in spirit if not in blood. This was not what attracted me to her but I appreciated it more once I saw her through my father's eyes. She loved him too so it didn't surprise me that the story of his final hours pulled the air right out of her. I used to think about his last few hours almost constantly, then as time went on just several times a day, and now, six years later, only several times a week.

Dad died just as I was beginning an archaeological excavation in a remote area of New Mexico just a couple miles from the Mexican border. He had been diagnosed with cancer only a month earlier and the doctor said that it wouldn't be long, maybe a couple of months, maybe less, maybe more. He had been in and out of the Veteran's hospital and I had visited several times in the past month, making the 500 mile trip to the U.P. from Illinois. I decided to get the field team started in New Mexico and then leave it to my co-director to run the excavation so that I could be with my mother, two sisters, wife and two kids during this difficult period. Cell phones didn't work in the field so I was making a land line call from the ranch head quarters, ten miles down a dusty two-rut road from our excavation site. Becky gave me the grim news. He had taken a sudden turn for the worse and both my sisters had taken off work and were now by his side along with my mother. I was supposed to stay in New Mexico for another week but it was time for me to go home too.

After driving for seven hours, I rounded the corner in Iron Mountain, Michigan on May 20th, Armed Forces Day, and the large VA hospital blocked out the setting sun. Although I had pulled into the parking lot maybe a dozen times in the past month, I knew that this would be the last time. Part of me hoped that he had died during my trip but the other part of me wanted to see him one last time. I walked in the room that smelled of death from the cancer that had now spread into his lungs. "I think he was waiting for you," my mother said as she greeted me. My mother and two sisters seemed happy to see me if only because I broke up the routine of the death vigil that they had been holding by his bedside for the last five days. We all hugged and they looked quite exhausted and I was sorry that I hadn't been there with them these final days. Dad hadn't eaten, slept, or even closed his eyes in the past several days. His breathing was rapid and strong like a charging race horse despite the maximum amount of morphine given to him for the pain. He punched at the air like he was batting away a foe and when we held his hand he squeezed so hard that our fingers turned blue.

We took turns sitting beside his bed, holding his hand, and giving him sips of water. My mom and sisters had been on the death watch for six straight days already yet they all stayed with me during my first shift.

The doctor visited and said, "No fingerprint is the same and no two people die in the same way." Dad's way, of course, was to fight, but for his last days it was up to his subconscious to do battle. Native American warriors of old yearned for a "good death," one that came in battle. My father, punching at the air, chose to die in combat with an enemy visible only to himself. He was badly weakened by days without food or sleep yet he put up a gallant fight. It would be a good death. I grabbed his hand and told him gently, "It's alright," but he squeezed my fingers so tight that I had to pry them free. It was hard to watch.

The clock said 2:00 a.m. but it didn't really matter as life now revolved around three hour shifts at my dad's bedside. I got up occasionally and walked around the room to stretch my legs but my eyes never left him. I prayed that it would end soon but then recanted and prayed that it would never end.

"So what is going to happen when he dies," I asked the hospice nurse who had seen death countless times.

"His breathing will get shallower and shallower and then finally stop." Instead of shallower more infrequent breathing, his was faster and deeper each hour. The confused look on my face made her shrug her shoulders. "He's a fighter."

A little after 2:00 a.m. his breathing slowed a bit and he seemed more restful. My older sister, Mary Fran, couldn't sleep so she was in the room during my watch.

"Maybe I should get mom and Karen."

"Maybe," I whispered.

She patted me on the shoulder and walked out of the room. I grabbed his hand, leaned close and whispered, "I love you, dad. You're my hero, you know." He sat up straight in bed, squeezed my hand like a vice, his face grimacing in the final violent struggle. He rested back down just as my mom and sisters came in. My mom crawled in bed with him and stroked his face but his large powerful hand still held me tightly. He took his final breath. It was a good death.

That was only the second time I had told him I loved him, the first was 10 days earlier just before I left for New Mexico. He told me he loved me too. This was not something men of his generation often did in this part of the world, but I needed to do it and I could tell that he did too. Both of us fought back tears as I walked out of the room and down the six flights of stairs. I drove away but had to stop along the road to collect myself. I tell my own son and daughter that I love them everyday, sometimes twice per day. I suppose this might be an over reaction as the expression can easily become a cliche, like "see ya," or "have a nice day." But something deep within drives me to say it anyway. It may mean less to my kids who say in response, "Love you too," but it never means less to me.

Now three days later we were in the first pew, quite numb, watching him lay there in silence. It seemed wrong that complete strangers had been with him these last three days; dressing him in his suit, combing his hair, placing his powerful hands just so. Beside me was my wife Becky, our daughter Sadie, and our son, Matt, named after his grandpa. On the other side of me was my mother, my sisters and their families. My mother seemed so small and fragile. She was like a freeze-dried rose and I was afraid that if I squeezed her too hard she might disintegrate into a pile of mournful dust. Each breath she took, each beat of her heart seemed to be painful. They were married in September of 1945, soon after Dad returned from the war. For the next 55 years of their lives they had done everything together—raised children, buried loved ones, built houses, traveled, and now said the final goodbye. Starting on this day the long duet was over and it seemed like her life might be too.

The long serpent of cars wound down a steep hill and across the Paint River as we made the short but slow trip to the cemetery. All traffic pulled to the curb as we past, people on the street stopped, some took their hats off while others put their hand over their heart. The cemetery was a beautiful place, filled with towering Norway pines that made a haunting whisper with only a gentle breeze. Evergreens, a symbol of eternal life, are in many cemeteries. In the 1930s my dad cut truck loads of pine boughs and hauled them to Chicago to sell to the Polish families who wanted to cover the graves of their loved ones in the winter; the blanket of evergreen branches providing a symbolic contrast to the snow-covered landscape. Everlasting life was certainly everyone's hope who buried their loved ones deep within the earth. A number of people in the past 24 hours had said to me, "He's in a better place." I would nod my head politely despite feeling that this was an absurd comment. The place he was in just a month ago seemed pretty good. The thing he loved most was to make his wife happy. On this day I'd never seen anyone so sad as my mother, her legs barely able to hold up her own weight. His choice would have been to stick around a while longer; that was the better place. My son was 11 years old and my daughter 8, I think a better place would have been for dad to take a drive with Matt at the wheel or to watch Sadie go off on her first date.

As we walked to his grave I was aware for the first time that it was a nice day, clear, sunny but still quite cool despite the fact that it was near the end of May. The grass was just getting green and was so heavy with dew that after just a few steps I could feel the dampness in my shoes. Dad's flag-draped coffin was carried over to the family plot, purchased years ago by my parents, which was near their parents, brothers and sisters. As I walked on this hallowed ground I passed some who died well before I was born and others I knew and loved.

There was my great uncle Walter Kubinski, who died in his mid-30s in 1917 from the flu during the famous epidemic that killed millions. Nearby was the grave of his sister, my dad's mother, who believed that God gave her a baby boy, my father, in 1917 to replace her beloved brother Walter. Remarkably, my grandmother and her sister had tickets on the *Titanic* in 1912 when first immigrating to the U.S., but they were bumped to another vessel, the *Kaiser Wilhelm der Grosse*, by people willing to pay more for the third class fare. The *Kaiser Wilhelm*, leaving from Bremen, Germany, had an earlier departure date and it arrived in New York 18 days before the sinking of the *Titanic*. Just two years later the *Kaiser Wilhelm* was taken over by the German Navy, outfitted with guns and is credited with sinking two British supply boats near the Canary Islands before it too was sunk in 1914 by the *HMS Highflyer*. As I stepped over their graves and their remarkable stories on this sacred ground, I thought of how ancestor worship is a large part of many traditional religions around the world. As my own father entered the ground it became for me the holiest of holy places, a shrine of greater importance than any found in Jerusalem or Mecca.

Family and friends shuffled in, no one talking above a whisper. The priest performed his final blessing and the American flag was removed from my father's poplar casket and presented to my mother. The color guard commander barked out his orders and five old soldiers readied their antique weapons. I could see spits of fire erupt from their rifles and the loud report of the guns made everyone flinch. As the last of the three gun blasts still echoed off the distant hills someone disappeared behind a nearby tree, pushed a button on a CD player and started taps. My nephew, just behind me, started to cry and the sound of quiet weeping cascaded through the crowd. I could see one of the color guardsmen biting his lip, staring hard at the horizon, fighting back tears.

After my dad's funeral, I stayed in the U.P. for a week or so and then spent several weeks in our home in Illinois before going back to New Mexico to finish out the archaeological excavation. I told my co-director that this was my last time at the site despite the fact that the project was to go for two more years. I needed to go home and excavate—start an archaeological project in the U.P. When my father went into the ground part of me died too, but something had sprung to life as well. I wanted to dig in the soil that my father loved and that now held him. I wanted to peel back the layers of time to reconstruct the past of this remarkable place and reflect on parts of his life that he never talked about. But I also needed to dig into my own soul, to explore my life and the feelings that had erupted as we placed him in the ground. We were so similar but so different too. He was a war hero and I was a war protester. I was against the war not in spite of him but because of him. He learned how to be a man from his father, I learned from him, and now I was teaching my own son. Four generations of fathers and sons and each quite different. Each generation tries to raise their children a little differently, in part because of the lessons taught to us by our parents and in part because of the different world that surrounds us.

My grandfather arrived in the U.S. when he was 19, encouraged to leave Poland by his father, who wanted his son to have a life free from military conscription and the bloody wars that had become part of life in southern Poland. Right after landing in New York he was lured to the U.P. by the mining companies, hungry for labor. His journey, filled with hardship yet opportunity, was quite different than my father's, raised in the Great Depression and sent back to Europe to fight the tyrants who his own father had fled. My journey to manhood occurs in the 1960s and 1970s where there were conflicting messages. I was intrigued by guns, warriors and warfare, but I saw firsthand the horrors of war from returning Vietnam veterans and the discussions, and lack thereof, of WWII by my father and his friends. The war in Iraq also inspired me to think about how war shaped our family history and how war and violence were part of growing up male in the U.P.

There are certain memorable moments in the journey toward manhood, and one such moment occurred long ago, in a little town on a hill in the winter of 1968.

*   *   *

The snow banks were high, well over my head, and I was tall for an eight almost nine year old. Our one village plow truck was a mammoth army surplus relic that couldn't go over 20 miles per hour. It took all of the driver's strength and both hands to turn its massive wheels. The truck snorted up and down the hills of our small town piling the snow ever higher as the streets got narrower after each storm. By winter's end the roads were wide enough for just one car, which was never a problem as two cars rarely passed regardless of the season.

The village truck also spread sand on the streets. The dump-box was filled with sand and a man would stand precariously on the heap and throw it on the road. This winter the village made a big purchase, a two-wheeled spreader that was pulled behind the truck. Now the man just had to shovel sand into the hopper and work the hand control that started and stopped the flow. The sander was a big improvement because the width of the road could be covered instead of the occasional splats of sand from the shovel-man. Sand was a necessity on our steep and slippery hills of our village, Alpha. It was common to see cars spinning to a stop on an incline, backing down the hill and either making another higher speed run at it or searching for a less slippery way to make it to their destination.

Learning to ride a bike was dangerous business on Alpha's streets because once you got the bike upright you were careening down a hill. The day after I learned to stay up on two wheels I took off down a hill, the pedals spinning faster than my legs so I couldn't put on the coaster breaks. I smashed into the Maki's car, breaking the taillight. I remember my dad carrying me home and putting me down on the couch as a golf ball size lump appeared on my forehead. Every kid in town had a similar story.

But the best part of the hills was that they were great for sledding. The new spreader, however, ruined the sledding because it spread the sand evenly. The splats of sand thrown down onto the road could be easily avoided by good sled driving, but our steel runners would come to a quick stop when they hit an unavoidable patch of sand made by the new spreader. Our favorite form of winter recreation was ruined until my dad saved the day. He convinced the village custodian and constable to discontinue sanding our hill despite the fact that it would make it impossible at times for cars to make the climb. He knew that there would be grumbling among some residents, but he surmised that it was safer for the kids to confine their sleigh riding to one hill instead of weaving among the cars on all the streets. And when our road became impassable, he argued, people could just use another, sanded, route.

Although "our hill" was technically 3rd St. and formed the eastern and northern boundaries of Alpha, we called it our hill because my house sat at the pinnacle of the best sledding in town. Our village custodian agreed not to sand the hill, and after the next snow storm the fastest sled run around was back.

We met there every night after dinner. It got dark around 4:00 p.m. but the hill had three street lights. It was more exhilarating to sled at night. The street lights were placed far enough apart so that we traveled in and out of darkness as we barreled down the slope. The colder night air made the road faster for our sleds and the shadows created by the distantly spaced street lights gave the run an eerie feel and added to the excitement.

From our kitchen window I could see a few kids already at the top of the hill under the first street light. I put on my wool pants, army replica winter jacket, leather "choppers" for my hands, and a ski mask that pulled down all the way to my shoulders and left only my face exposed.

The first few steps out on a cold night always made me want to turn back to the warmth of the house. And this was a cold night. There was no wind but the snow crunched like cornflakes under my boots. The first few breaths of arctic air brought an ache to my lungs before the cold started to penetrate my skin. I knew that I just had to make it through the first sled run as the walk up the hill in the heavy cloths would warm me up and make the frigid night tolerable. The sound traveled so well in the crisp air that I could almost make out the words of the banter from the small group of guys gathered on the hill under the street light. Above the crackle of snow beneath my feet I heard a single dog barking, who was soon joined by a second and third. By the location and sound of the dogs I knew their owners. Two of the dogs were friendly and they could be approached even when tied up. But there was no mistaking the third dog's bark, lower and a bit more menacing. This dog was so mean that no one went near it. I had a scar on my left calf from the last time he was loose. Only dogs and boys were out on this cold night.

Most of the regulars had come out tonight and each was two or three years older than me. I suppose I had two types of friends, violent ones and not so violent ones. Being a violent or rough friend didn't mean that you wanted to hurt anyone, only that you tended to get involved in activities that involved action, physical contact, competition, and maybe even a little bit of danger. All my friends climbed trees but my rough friends would dare each other to jump off the highest branch. We all swam but some of my friends would see who could hold their breath the longest under water, swim under a submerged log or do flips off the dock. These were the friends who ended up playing football or other competitive sports. The not-so-rough friends, who I enjoyed just as much, liked to play chess or checkers, build something out of wood, and ride a bike without having to construct a jump to see how far we could fly.

And it was mostly the rough group who was out sledding. It was hard to see their faces but I could tell who was there by their clothes, the way they walked, or the way they wore their hats. There was Joey, who was about my size but quite a bit stronger. He had a wiry kind of strength that permitted him to swing in trees like the monkeys at the Milwaukee County Zoo. His hair was as light as mine was dark. When he went swimming it went transparent, which made him look like his balding father. Joey was also the fastest and most daring sled rider. Even on the coldest nights his hat was always slightly askew and snow covered, a remnant of an earlier wipe out.

Raymond was the biggest kid in the group. He had several large, crusty warts on each hand, which he liked to stick with pins until they bled. Sometimes each wart had so many pins that they resembled mini pin cushions. He had a tendency toward meanness so I tried to stay clear of him if I could. He was the type of kid who blew up frogs with fire crackers and thought it was the funniest thing he ever saw. All of us liked to wrestle but whenever someone was pinned and cried "uncle" they were let up. If you screamed "uncle" to Raymond it was an invitation for more painful torture accompanied by his sickening cackle.

Cheetah was older than me but about my height yet, smaller and slightly fragile. He seemed to be sick a lot and he was prone to go home after several runs especially if he was involved in a big wipe out. He liked the violent games but didn't have the body for it. He often had a significant injury of some sort like a broken arm or some undisclosed malady that required frequent trips to the doctor. He wore ill-fitted glasses that were always sliding down his nose. Cheetah always seemed a little bit insecure and unsteady, except when he ran. The only thing faster in our town were the dogs, and even they seemed to respect Cheetah's speed. When he was hanging out he always seemed uncomfortable in his own skin, uneasy and fidgety. But when he ran, as he sliced through the air like a knife, he was confident and happy. He seemed to move his legs twice as fast as anybody else.

And finally there was Richie, the comedian of the group who always made me laugh especially when he told a deliciously dirty joke. Richie's was best at imitating voices of people at school and around town. He could imitate some of our teachers so perfectly that if you closed your eyes you would think that they were telling dirty jokes, which made even the bad jokes funny.

They greeted me as I came out of the shadows. They already had several runs of "war" in. When there were two or more kids on the hill we played war. We divided up the teams so there was an even number of older and younger kids on each team. It was a simple yet exhilarating game. The first group took off and the other chased them down the hill. The objective was to make it down the hill without being caught. Skilled drivers could weave back and forth and artfully aim for the faster parts of the road. We road the sleds on our bellies and had great control by bending the front handle left or right and dragging a toe if necessary, although that slowed you down. The older broken in sleds were the best because the driver could bend the entire sled and turn it with remarkable precision. My sled, which was not even a year old, was kind of stiff and not the best at turning but it ran fast and true.

The pursuers took off a couple of seconds later and tried to catch sleds ahead of them and force a wipe-out. Sometimes if the lead sleds were caught they would turn harmlessly sideways and both sleds would come to a gentle stop, but in most cases the captured sled would suffer a more violent end. The worst case scenario, for the lead sled, was to have an attacker get a firm hold of boots or back runners and send the person flying into the snow bank, which on cold nights was hard as rock, or they could push a sled sideways into the path of riders causing a bone crunching pile up. The lead sleds, however, were not defenseless as they could kick their legs at their attacker's head and arms hoping to send them careening out of control. As one of the younger, smaller kids on the hill I rarely could fend off an attacker once they had me, but even someone as small as me could occasionally, as an attack sled, send an older kid smashing into the bank, which made it fairer than alot of games we played.

I was chosen as one of the three sleds to be attacked. Someone in back shouted, "Ready, Go!" but I was already off. Jumping the start was a serious violation and I heard the protests as I took my four running steps and slammed my sled down on the ice. I was too cold to get pummeled into the snowbank on my first run so I insured that I made it down without incident. Richie did too but Raymond caught Joey and I turned in time to see him smash into the icy bank, with Raymond laughing like he just blew up a frog. Instead of coming to a sudden bone jarring stop, Joey's runners hit a gentle slope that rocketed him over the bank into deep snow on the other side.

"Cool!" I heard someone yell. By the time we made it to the bottom of the hill Joey was already standing, his wool pants and coat covered in snow. He shook the snow off his hat, put it back on again askew, and hopped on his sled and rode slowly down the rest of the hill to his awaiting admirers.

Each of us took turns reviewing Joey's flight with these types of comments.

"Did you fly or what!"

"I bet you went 10 feet in the air!"

After each of these comments we always did the same thing, which was sort of like some ancient ritual resurrected for great feats such as this. It reminded me a little of the laughing hyenas I had seen on the nature shows. We stood in a circle with big toothy grins and each comment was followed by nodding in agreement while making a cackling noise that was a cross between laughing and grunting. After we all had chance to make an admiring remark, it was time for Joey and Raymond to relive the event. This was met with more smiling, cackling and nodding as we made our way back up the hill. We got to the point of the crash and paced off the distance he had flown and did more nodding and cackling. Joey was the envy of the group. It was a place of honor to be the recipient of the cackling and nodding. We lived for the big crashes, and looking around at the broken front teeth in our smiling group you could tell that they all had similar stories.

Three out of the six sled riders had one or more cracked front teeth, and I was proudly there when most of them were broken. Chipped front teeth were such a town problem that it was a common topic for my mother's coffee clutch or the daily gatherings at the post office. They talked about the tooth chipping problem all winter but had no real solution.

"I think it looks cool" I told my mom one day after she pleaded with me to watch out for my teeth. "Ray Nitschke has no front teeth and he is the greatest middle linebacker who ever lived."

"Jimmy! It is not cool, it ruins your smile. You watch your teeth when you play," she scolded.

I saw teeth get broken in such different situations that I knew there was no real way to stop it. Some were chipped during hockey games at the skating rink, some were damaged by a rock or a baseball bat, and others occurred during sled wars. They became someone's unique signature and I secretly wished I had at least one small chip. Maybe my mom's warning as I went outdoors, "Watch your teeth," really did have an effect because all my teeth were intact.

A chipped tooth was a sign of great courage and a permanent souvenir of former battles. It looked tough, cool, and mean. If you asked the kid about it he would break into an elaborate exciting story. Like a snowflake, each chipped tooth was unique. Some were diagonal, some horizontal, and some involved both teeth. My favorite look was a diagonal chip of one tooth and the other tooth unchipped but black and dead from some vicious blow.

No two chips were the same but the chipping experience fell into two extremes: terrible pain, and not even knowing that your tooth was chipped. The painful variety usually involved a cut lip and lots of blood. Luckily there was usually a ready supply of ice. Bloody snowballs used on a smashed mouth might last for weeks on the side of the road. But the other no pain variety happened just as often. My dad explained that cold teeth break easily—like an icicle snapping. After a nasty pile up we would all be laughing and someone might feel something in their mouth, like a small piece of ice had flown in during the crash. They would spit the tooth chip on the ground or in their hand without even knowing it had happened. Even after their tongue had found the broken tooth they had to get someone to look at their mouth to confirm the break. All my sledding buddies, once they left Alpha for college or jobs, eventually got their teeth capped and their smiles restored to their mother's satisfaction but ruining their character, in my opinion.

We took several more runs down the hill that night without anymore memorable crashes. The worst was when someone in the lead group was spun out of control and I crashed into them. Even though we were all wearing several inches of winter clothes that made excellent padding, getting hit with the steel front of a sled caused a nasty bruise. Our arms and legs were covered with purple and yellow patches from former crashes. The kid I hit, Cheetah, got the worst of it, a direct hit from my sled into his upper arm, and I rolled harmlessly over the top of him and skidded to a stop. Mercifully, none of the riders plowed into me as I lay defenseless on the road. I hopped back on my sled and finished off the ride but Cheetah decided to stay mid-hill, compose himself, and wait for the other riders to pick him up on their way back up the hill.

On this walk up the hill, Joey had some news. Bobby and Buddy went down the Bear Cave Hill on a toboggan last weekend. According to Joey, they went right off the jump and smashed a toboggan into a million pieces.

We all listened with great interest as Joey told us all he knew about this latest trip down the infamous Bear Cave Hill. Bobby and Buddy were teenagers and they were the latest to go down the hill. No one in our party had been down the hill but it was a rite of passage that we knew we would all have to make at some point. No boy could officially become a man without that fateful ride. This activity was forbidden by all parents so it was done secretly and in small groups so as not to attract attention.

We had all been up the hill many times, but only in summer. A trip to the hill in June or July was like a pilgrimage to a holy site. If you walked without too many stops you could get to the top in about an hour, but for most of us it was a half day event. Last summer, a city friend, Steven, and I had to stop by the creek and catch frogs, throw rocks into the pond, and climb a tree or two along the way. Once we got to the hill we made three stops. The first was the actual Bear Cave. My dad was the first to take my sisters and me to the cave, and I was so young that I had to be carried some of the way. The cave was a hollowed out rock shelter in the side of the hill.

"Does a bear really live here?" I asked my dad on the first visit with more than a little fear in my voice.

"I suppose they could hibernate here in the winter," my dad replied.

"A bear made this cave?" I wondered.

"No, no, this was made by the mining company."

We lived in a mining town in Michigan's Upper Peninsula and two iron ore mines had once been in operation. The last one closed not long after I was born. The woods and fields surrounding our town had numerous small test holes about the size of a car. My dad could always tell one that was made by the mining company even though they were now filled with trees and completely grown over.

"Nature doesn't make holes like that," he explained.

Although I realized that no bear made the cave and probably ever lived in it, walking into the cool, dark, and damp shelter always made the hair stand up on my neck. It was unlike any place I knew. Several people had carved their initials in the moss growing on the back wall's jagged rock. Water dripped out of the cracks in a couple of places forming small pools of water that was ice-cold to the touch. We saw a few beer cans on the floor during our last summer trip and we tried to make up a story about how they got there. Steven and I concluded that it was probably some highschool kids who snuck up here with some beer. The fire ring near the mouth of the cave added to the story.

I was glad when we left the cave for our second stop, the skeleton of a shattered toboggan. It was hard to find, half buried in the grass and weeds, but we always looked at it and cleared away some of the vegetation. A small tree, too big to pull out, had now taken root between its broken, faded boards. We sat on what remained of the sled and pretended we were rocketing down the hill, which loomed behind us. The toboggan was well off the hill into the woods and we shuddered at the thought of two or three anonymous boys who took this fateful ride. There were so many stories about broken toboggans that we had no way of matching this one to any of the stories. My mouth went dry thinking of me on this toboggan.

After spending some time in the toboggan graveyard, it was time to get to the real reason for coming—the hill and jump. This was no ordinary hill, it was altered to make an actual ski jump. I had never seen it officially used, but my father, who was born and raised in Alpha, vaguely recalled ski jumpers going off the hill. Several towns in the area had ski jumps, big and small, that were still in use. These were all immense structures constructed of wood and metal and were the sites of amazing bravery and daring. We had such sharp, steep hills in Alpha that they built a ski jump right on the side of the hill. This was not a big ski jump hill, there were certainly bigger ones, but it was not the smallest one I had seen either. The Finns and the Swedes did most of the ski jumping, a tradition that they brought from their homeland. If your family was into this type of thing, you started young going off small jumps and gradually worked up to the gigantic sky flying hills in Iron Mountain or Ironwood. Jerry Martin won most of the events at these hills and was an alternate on the 1968 U.S. Olympic ski jump team in Grenoble, France, and he did make the team in 1972 and 1976. I recall him in particular because he wore an eyepatch over a blind eye giving him the fearless look of a pirate.

We trudged up the hill away from the toboggan skeleton until we got to the jump, which must have been constructed by a bulldozer. "Nature doesn't make bumps like this one," I guessed, thinking of my dad. Steven and I stood on the edge of the jump and stared upward in reverent awe at the hill before us. From where we were standing it seemed straight up.

The final thing to do, of course, was to climb the hill. This required walking sideways, leaning into the hill and pulling yourself up by grabbing onto the small aspen trees that had sprouted in the spring. We climbed with determination and were hot and sweaty by the time we reached the top. We sat and dug our heels in so as not to slide down and pondered what it would be like to shoot down this mountain. On the entire walk to the hill we had talked bravely about how we would go down the hill the following winter. This conversation happened for three straight summers and it was the view from the top of the hill that usually changed our minds. From this point of view, it seemed like a free fall and certain death. We had to crane our necks out a bit just to see the base of the jump. And the path down the hill, only about the width of a car, was lined with trees that seemed to grow closer every year.

The view, besides being terrifying, was spectacular. I felt like a bird among the clouds and there was always a steady breeze even on a windless day. The cool breeze chased the sweat out of our clothes and reminded us of the icy chill of winter. Our perch also gave us a unique perspective on Alpha. We could identify all the houses. My house, on top of the hill across the valley was in clear view, though it was obscured some by the leaves of our maple trees in the backyard. From this vantage point you could tell that many of the houses were almost identical mining company houses. From a distance it was hard to tell them apart but once you got close you could see how each had its own personality. Each owner had made changes to the house to give them their own touch; a covered front porch, a willow tree, climbing vine or a color other than white.

"Houses are a lot like people," I told Steven. "From a distance they all look the same but when you get close you see that they are all very different."

"I guess," Steven replied while giving me a push causing me to grip the grass to keep from sliding down the hill.

On the walk home I wondered if I would ever have the courage to go down Bear Cave Hill. The welcome distraction of the creek, skipping rocks and catching frogs, helped to settle my mind and set the looming challenge behind me for awhile. But once I got home, Bear Cave Hill was in full view from my kitchen window. It haunted me daily yet seemed so small and insignificant from the haven of my home. It was just a thin break in the trees on the hill across the valley. The jump was not visible nor could one comprehend the steepness of the grade and the fear one had when sitting on the top. A shudder ran through my body as I turned away from the hill and the whisper of a voice that every boy in Alpha heard each winter.

"Ride me."

The winter of 1968 would indeed be the winter that I would ride down Bear Cave Hill. My first step toward manhood.

Chapter 2

Garden Run

"And that's the way it is," Walter Cronkite told us all every night on the *CBS Evening News*. Magically beaming in from the tower antennae erected on the side of our house came three channels on our brand new color TV, 12 (NBC), 6 (CBS), and 13 (PBS) but we only watched Walter Cronkite and Channel 6 for the news. If I was at someone else's house around dinner time it was possible, but rare, that Huntley and Brinkley on Channel 12 would be on but they were intruders in our house. Channel 12, coming out of Green Bay, also didn't come in too well unless you adjusted the direction of the antennae, which you did remotely by pushing the "South" button on the small brown box collecting dust on the floor behind the TV. CNN and the all news channels have certainly ruined the drama and importance of the nightly news. Back then, our dinner time and all other evening activities were planned around watching Walter Cronkite.

That's the way it might be, according to Cronkite, but it didn't mean my parents had to like it. In 1968 several of Alpha's boys were challenging their manhood in Vietnam, and the news each evening would report the body count, how many Americans and Viet Cong had been killed and wounded. This year was especially bloody as the military launched the Tet offensive, and the number of Americans killed seemed to grow larger each day. My mother sighed and my father scowled each night as "Uncle Walter" gave the death toll. The numbers were often like 38 American and 127 North Vietnamese dead and hundreds more wounded. We now know that the number of Viet Cong killed was exaggerated but at the time it made it sound, especially to a young boy, that we were winning big. It was more like he was announcing the Packer and Bear score to me, and I was excited that we were killing them. If I let my enthusiasm spill out, however, by saying something like, "We sure are cream'en um," my mother would remark

16

coldly, left eye brow raised in disappointment, that there were 38 mothers without their sons tonight.

My place during "news time" was often laying on my back on the floor next to my dad. He seemed to prefer the floor where he could stretch out his back or maybe even take a short post-dinner cat nap right after the news. I liked the couch better but not enough to give up a spot on the floor next to him. He would often reach over and grab my knee or slyly put his big hand under my chin for a surprise tickle. On many of the nights when the news was bad, however, he just laid there and scowled at the TV, his body tense and unmoving. He had a serious look, which some people might call mean. When he was serious or just concentrating, his eyes narrowed slightly and the flesh would fold, in two creases, between his eyes in a look that Mrs. Hammacher, my 3rd grade teacher, called a "furrowed brow." "Un-furrow your brow," she would say sternly as she listened to me read aloud in class.

Once a source of enjoyment and a connection to the bigger world, news had lately become the most stressful half hour of the day, complete with furrowed brows and the absence of tickling. I usually loved the news. It was exciting to see people and places around the world, pictures from space, and movie stars, but the reports from Vietnam sucked the joy out of our living room. With the sound of gunfire in the background reporters huddled in fox holes or behind bullet-scared walls telling us about the advance of troops. Occasionally, a rocket dropped close by causing the reporter to flinch along with me and the rest of my family in our living room. I imagined everyone in town, except the few watching channel 12, jumped at the same time too. A bomb goes off in a little village thousands of miles away and everyone in our little village flinches. Our TV certainly made the world seem smaller.

I suppose that it was one of the worst times to get a color TV. Ever since we got it the previous January there seemed to be nothing but violent news, all in living color. Assassinations, race riots, cities burning, violence at the Democratic National Convention, Miss America Pageant protested by women's "libbers," war protests and violence on campus, and the blood from the battlefield all became more vivid with our new Montgomery Ward TV. Mom and dad always had to tell us to back away from the set because of the fear of being exposed to too much radiation from the color TV, but it also seemed that they wanted to distance us from the news and the tragedy of the outside world.

As an archaeologist who studies technology and change, I wonder how much the color TV in everyone's living room may have actually played a role in the social and political changes during this time. It is one thing to read about student violence on campus, but it is another to see a policeman club someone on the head or to witness a crowd being moved with tear gas and fire hoses. Our television and movie screens today are filled with realistic violence but in the late 1960s the most terror I was likely to see on daily TV was when Lassie fell into a hole and was temporarily knocked unconscious. The vivid violence of the TV news was a dramatic contrast to the rest of the TV world, and as this device became part of everyone's living room I suspect that it played as significant a role in social change for the day as the introduction of any ancient technology. One of my favorite technologies is pottery, which first appeared in North America about in 2000 BC in the southeastern U.S. The first pottery in North America was part of a technological and dietary change that altered the world of prehistoric Native Americans forever. TV in the late 1960s played a similar role as both are a result of and a catalyst for change.

But technological change today comes much more rapidly and we struggle to keep pace. There is a common notion that technological change is progress, but any archaeologist will tell you that change is just change and can be good or bad depending upon your perspective. A recent example is the cell phone, which suddenly has become so prevalent that even junior high age kids have them in their pocket or purse. My wife and I were at my son's baseball game several years ago and we, along with most parents, were actively engaged in cheering on our kids as they tried their best to hit and catch the ball. One dad, however, caught my eye as he spent the entire game on his cell phone. He might think of his cell phone as a technological advancement permitting him to attend his son's game while making some of his business calls. But certainly you could also argue that cell phone use behavior of this kind is actually a step backward; most people would agree that talking on the phone instead of watching your son play ball seems to be quite unacceptable. On campus I often see two or three friends walking through the quad side-by-side, each one talking on the cell phone to distant friends but not to the people right beside them. Technology can change our world but is it progress?

The television certainly had an impact on our world, but as a young boy I, unlike my parents, wasn't depressed by the news at all. Just like the college-age cell phone users of today who see nothing wrong with their use of this technology, I found the TV and especially the news exciting and full of adventure. The year 1968 brought us the first live images from space and I watched in awe, dreaming, like most kids, of one day becoming an astronaut. And what young man didn't find the woman's movement exciting. I watched with fascination as young women liberated themselves from their bras and tossed them into a fire. Even the war news and the body count, which my parents found especially stressful because we knew several boys in the war from Alpha, I thought was exciting. I thought it wonderful that they were in the war, seeing the world, dressing in the cool GI Joe clothes, and shooting guns. I, along with many of my friends, loved everything about war. The acts of bravery, adventure, living in the wilderness, and hunting down the enemy were all exciting and wonderful. From the look on my parents' faces I would guess that they did not share my enthusiasm and excitement, and I really didn't understand why.

My mother collected information about the war in different ways. One way was at the almost daily coffee clutches, sometimes done by phone, and another was at the post-office, where a small group of people gathered right when all the mail was put out. The post-office was a converted gas station, and you could still see the spot in the front where the gas pump once sat. We had box 57, which we opened with great anticipation each day with the lock combination, "three times to J, two times to B, and in-between C and D." Mr. Leonardi, the Postmaster, was about my dad's age but had a mop of wavy hair and a little mustache that he kept neatly trimmed. He was quick with advice regarding all things from when to plant your tomatoes to who to vote for in an upcoming election. And for every possible situation he seemed to have an appropriate saying.

"A penney saved is a penney earned."

"A bird in the hand is worth two in the bush."

On school days after the first rush of town's people a few of us sometimes hung out in the post-office before the bell rang, especially on the cold days. Mr. Leonardi might quiz us about our studies and if we were unresponsive he would grab one of our books and ask us questions about history, science or math. If someone was carrying a band instrument he sometimes made them play a tune. He would close his eyes, listening intently, head swaying gently to the rhythm of some squeaky, off-key song. When they finished he would tersely say, "Good, keep practicing." Once there was a clarinet in the group and he grabbed it and filled the post-office with notes better than had been produced by any of us.

Mr. Leonardi opened the doors around 8:00, or as soon as he got out all the mail. By then a small group of people would congregate in front of the post-office and enter when he unlatched the door for those eager to collect their mail and the local news. I knew that there was no bad news about the boys in the war or anything else tragic or exciting if they talked about the weather right off the bat, giving Mr. Leonardi a chance to give us his latest wisdom, possibly extracted from a Farmer's Almanac kept hidden behind the counter.

If you missed this most informative first group at the post-office, which we rarely did, it was Mr. Leonardi's duty to distribute the daily report, which is a job he did with enthusiasm and an official sense of urgency. Sometimes the mood was light and there might be some laughing among the patrons but Mr. Leonardi took his job seriously, which gave the place a somber mood. He was the only U.S. Government employee in town and he made sure that the place was run in a way that would make President Lyndon B. Johnson proud, whose framed picture gazed down on us from the wall next to the poster that scolded us to "Remember

Our Boys." Alpha didn't need much reminding. With a town this small, made up mostly of inter-married lineages, nearly everyone in town was related to at least one of the boys serving in the war.

The final place that my mother and others collected news was at Hoholek's, the only store in town. Hoholek's was located on the opposite side of town from our house but took just a couple minutes by car even at the snail's pace that most people drove. A drive through town was more like a leisurely stroll where you can look at the yards and wave at everyone you meet. The houses were small but no one seemed to notice. Most houses had a backyard garage that you got to from the alley, which saw more bike riding and ball playing than car traffic. The only big house in town had been built for the captain of Alpha's first iron ore mine, the Judson. It was a massive two and half story house on the edge of town on an enormous lot.

It was winter, so there was less to look at on our drive across town but speeds were still slow in part because this was the time of year that the encroaching snow banks made the roads one-lane and they were covered mostly of packed slippery snow, with a little sand sprinkled on.

Our town was like any of the dozens of about the same size that sprung up since the late 1800s anywhere a rich deposit of iron ore was found. We had two mines, the Judson, which opened up in the late 1800s and was responsible for founding our town, and the Book mine that closed just after I was born. There was always hope that another would open up again soon but with each passing year people seemed to realize that the bigger more efficient mines in other towns were there to stay. Many men from our town commuted the 60 or so miles one way each day to work in the mines.

Alpha was a mining town like all the others near us but it looked distinctly different. Other towns were either built in an almost random pattern with the roads following "old cow paths," or they were laid out in an unimaginative grid, so that every road either traveled north-south or east-west. The mining companies planned the town and built many of the first houses so they had the control of how the town would look forever. I liked to imagine that our town was designed by a frustrated artist because our streets were not laid out in the usual pattern. Maybe he was a painter who couldn't get any work so he took a job in the town planning division of the mining company in Boston or New York.

Our town from above would look like a wagon wheel cut off just above the hub with five spokes serving as our streets, made wide and grand despite the fact that it was designed before the time of cars. The hub was the "civic circle," where all the streets met and cars merged onto the road by turning right, following the circle and then exiting at their street of choice. Rarely did I ever see more than one car on the circle but it was a great way to control traffic, which was necessary during our town's boom years. Our civic circle is similar to a European "round-about" common in England and France prior to the invention of the stop light. I often wondered whether our frustrated town designer and artist had studied in France before taking a sensible job with the mining company. The first postmasters usually picked a town name, which were usually either named after a mining executive or more likely some local landmark, like Iron River, Crystal Falls, or Iron Mountain; all very ordinary and predictable names. But our town, Alpha, was named for the first letter of the Greek alphabet. Maybe our frustrated artist, who got the job to design Alpha, was inspired by the name to create a masterpiece, maybe working late into the night sipping wine and smoking cigarettes in his cramped Boston apartment.

Boom mining towns rise up instantly and then die slowly unless they find some other means to employ the local people. Logging and tourism saved many of the local towns but Alpha, slowing decaying since the Book mine closed in the early 1960s, has never found its niche. Even in the 1960s everyone knew it was dying and my parents and other town's people would often remind us that there was a life outside of Alpha and jobs outside the mines. The first postmaster and the town designer of old, giving the town a Greek name and French or English design, quietly gave this same message. It certainly helped me dream.

Driving to the store this morning with my mom we entered the civic circle, with its towering pine trees in the center, and I imagined our first postmaster living in a one room log house in 1888 and reading about ancient Greece in the evenings, and our French town designer, making technical sketches of small towns while his water colors hung on the wall unfinished. We passed the post office, Mr. Leonardi in plain sight through the window reporting the day's news to a small attentive audience, and as we rounded the corner I looked at our school, silent during winter vacation. The school, on the north end of the half wagon wheel hub, was next to the Township Hall, the water tank, and the fire hall, manned by 20 or so volunteer firemen. As we followed the curve around the civic circle we passed Scaritis Sinclair gas station with the green dinosaur on the glass top of the single gas pump, the VFW, and the Credit Union, where my sisters and I had our "college savings," which was the only way to realize these small town dreams. Exiting the circle we drove past the village tavern, located conveniently right next to the Catholic church, St. Edward, the patron saint of difficult marriages.

We were all baptized in this church, captured forever by my dad's Bell and Howell camera, with its blazing lights making everyone squint unnaturally for the event. We went to church every Sunday and almost everyday during lent. The part I liked best about the church was the stained glass windows. They were so beautiful but so out of place in our little mining town. They were our only real art

and each of the masterpieces had the name of a local family, most of whom I recognized: "In Memory of P. DeAmici," or "Donated by the Mr. and Mrs.
Wodjac."

When the church was built my grandfather refused to buy a window, which
may have had something to do with his efforts to develop the local "Polish
Catholic Church" that he along with other dedicated Pols built and maintained.
They would pay some local priest, who could speak Polish, to do mass at the
church once a month on Sunday afternoon after he had already completed his
parish's obligations. The mass was followed by dinner and dancing. The first
priest assigned to Alpha's Roman Catholic Church, Fr. Gondeck, built a lot of it
with his own two hands and the help of weary miners after their shift let out. It
was clear that he did not approve of this local breakaway of the Roman Catholic
church and most Polish families including ours no longer attended the Polish
Catholic Church. It lingered on for a time but then closed. It sat vacant for a long
while but has been taken over by an evangelical Christian group who must find it
easy to save Alpha's souls as St. Edwards also succumbed to the town's decay and
closed its doors after more than 75 years.

Past the Catholic church, without a window with our family name, we came
to Hoholek's store, which was owned by my aunt and uncle. I looked forward to
trips to the store. The building was originally a hotel, but my grandparents
bought it and made it into a dance hall right before the war. My parent's wedding
reception was held in the same room that now housed the store's goods. My
grandparents turned it into a variety store and my own mother was one of the
first clerks. Today, my aunt was working the register when we came in, which was
announced by the familiar jingle of the door.

My mom visited for awhile with my aunt, my dad's sister, and I was left to
wander up an down the rows. We, along with much of the town, did lots of our
shopping in the bigger stores in nearby towns but we always had an excuse to visit
the store once or twice a week. It was certainly unlike the bigger stores in Iron
Mountain. Although it had the usual groceries, milk, cereal, canned goods, fruits
and vegetables, it also had a wonderful assortment of items not found in the city
stores. Most of these more interesting items were in the back aisle, where I spent
most of my time. Not much shopping was done here anymore and I noticed
when an item had been purchased as an imprint was left of its shape on the dust
covered shelves. Here you could find hammers and nails, boots, socks, raincoats,
chains, axes, and even guns and ammo. My father said that he bought his first
gun here, from his father who then owned the store. The rifles, shotguns and
small 22s were hung on the wall and I spent a lot of time admiring them and
imagining myself sneaking through the woods hunting squirrels and rabbits.

My first gun was a Daisy BB gun, which really wasn't a real rifle. It shot the BB with forced air, which you compressed by "cocking" the lever. The best place to try out our weapons on live targets was at our rat invested town dump located on the edge of town. Every Wednesday the plow truck became the garbage hauler. One man heaved the cans to another standing in the open box. He simply emptied the can and tossed it to the ground. The morning after garbage day was the best time to hunt for rats. The only weapons my friends and I were allowed to shoot were our sling shots and BB guns. We couldn't kill a rat but making a direct hit was a thrill. A rat nailed with our weapons would jump or even do a complete flip before scurrying off behind the soup can or bike wheel that had just been picked up at the curb. Occasionally, a teenager with a 22 would be out at the dump. Their gun seemed like a cannon compared to our little weapons. You could tell that they were good shots because the dump always had the added stench of rotting flesh, the result of earlier rat killing expeditions. The garbage men ignited the trash each Wednesday but it only smoldered and sputtered giving off a putrid smell that always clung to your clothes.

I eventually got so good at shooting my Daisy rifle that I could hit a half dollar at 20 paces. I was bragging to my dad about my great skill just when a chipmunk popped up on the nearby woodpile. "I bet I can even hit that chipmunk," I bragged.

"No way," my dad replied. It was only about 25 paces away and I was sure I could hit it. I had watched the chipmunk since it was a baby and you could almost always see it scampering around the wood pile.

"You don't think I can hit that?" I asked with just a little bravado.

"No way," my dad said again. "That chipmunk is too far away and those guns are not that accurate." I thought otherwise.

"Want me to try?"

"Go right ahead," my dad replied honestly thinking that I didn't have a chance.

I cocked the lever action once and put the gun up to my shoulder, rested the side of my face against the cool metal, closed one eye and took aim. The chipmunk was sitting on his haunches using his two front paws to hold a seed that he was nervously eating. I took a deep breath, pulled the trigger and watched the BB travel straight towards the chipmunk—a direct hit.

"Wow," is all my dad said. We sat there for awhile watching the poor animal twitch. I must have hit it in the spine. My heart sunk. My dad soon got up, seemingly unfazed, and continued his chores and I walked over to the pile of wood. Mercifully, for me, the chipmunk's twitching had caused it to fall down into a crack out of sight but I could still hear it struggling, its claws rapping against the wood.

Once I demonstrated my skill with the Daisy rifle, my dad started to show me how to use a real gun. I was too young to carry a gun on my own but we went target shooting occasionally if I wore him down enough with my pestering. I loved the way the gun felt in my hand. The stock was sanded smooth and the barrel cool to the touch. Holding it made me feel grown up and powerful. It was surprisingly heavy and I could feel its power when I held it in my hand. I loved the sound it made when the shell ejected, the kick the gun made when fired, and the acrid smell of gun smoke that would hover in the air. It was mysterious and wonderful to me that I could pull the trigger on the gun and 50 yards away it would unleash its fury. On weekends sometimes we set up tin cans or bottles in the woods behind our house and my dad let me shoot his 22 until I had hit them all. When we walked to the targets I marveled at the way a small bullet could do such damage. More cans and bottles were set up and we would do it again. I missed more than I hit the targets and my dad would announce, "Too far to the left," or "Too high again," and I would try to make the correction. I could never tell where the missed bullets went. He had eyes like Superman. Sometimes he took a few shots to see if the gun was firing straight. Every shot hit the target.

"Did you learn to shoot that good aiming at Germans?" I inquired. I was always trying to get him to talk about the war, which he rarely did.

"I learned to shoot that straight by shooting at rabbits," my dad replied dryly.

I could shoot all day but finally my dad would say, "Bullets cost money, you know," and the fun would be over.

My grandpa gave me an old 410 shotgun, which, like the 22 caliber rifle, was a starter gun. This seemed more like a real gun to me as it gave an enormous report and the kick knocked me back slightly and made my shoulder ache. My dad taught me how to clean it and I did it everyday until he told me that the inside of the gun really doesn't get dirty unless it is fired. But I sat for hours with it, feeling its smooth grain wood stock and well-machined barrel.

At age 12 I took a gun safety class sponsored by the National Rifle Association. They taught us proper gun safety and took us target shooting, but by then I was already an accomplished marksman. I shot my first partridge with the 410 the following fall when I could first legally hunt. My dad and I crawled on our bellies close enough to a big elm tree where two birds were getting ready to roost for the night. With the sun setting, I got on my knees and shot one of the birds out of the tree. I just winged it, however, so it was flopping and running around near the base of the tree. "Should I shoot it again?" I asked.

"No, it will ruin the meat," my dad replied. "Put down your gun and help me catch it." I put down my gun but I had no intention of grabbing the crazed bird. Within seconds my dad caught the bird and twisted off his head with one quick turn of his wrist. This kill was worthy of a picture. When we got back home I stood next to the garage, gun in one hand, headless bird in the other as my mother snapped the shot.

By the time I shot my first deer I had killed lots of animals. With practice, it didn't bother me anymore. Farm kids like my dad are even more casual about killing things. My dad could put a bullet right into the head of a pig, steer, or lamb without even flinching though it made me a little squeamish.

"Isn't it hard to shoot them like that? I asked.

"Not really. It's really a humane way to put them down. Your grandpa, on the other hand, never wanted to waste a bullet on a farm animal so he would hit them in the head with a hammer. That seemed a little cruel to me because some of these steers have thick heads so he'd have to wack them several times while I tried to hold them still. I'd rather waste a bullet and I bet you would rather not have to hold the animal down while I beat it on the head." He was right about that.

"Your grandpa was something when he was younger. He wouldn't waste a second bullet on farm animal but he didn't mind firing a shot or two at people." I knew the story he was talking about, which he re-told on many occasions.

One Sunday a month during the summer and fall, the Polish families, many of them relatives, would gather for a dance. Although it was supposed to alternate between families, my grandparents liked to throw a party and even built a portable wood dance floor for the occasion. An uncle played the concertina and they danced and celebrated well into the evening, lubricated by the home-made moonshine. It was the Depression and Prohibition, but many of the families, including my grandparents, operated a still. By the time my father was a teenager, he had several younger sisters who apparently, during this summer, had started to "blossom." Two young men appeared uninvited at the party no doubt interested in my grandfather's young daughters. They overstayed their welcome and my grandfather asked them to leave. As they were getting into their car, a three cylinder, two-seat Duryea, they mouthed off to my grandfather who turned to my father and said, "Get the gun." All farmers kept a loaded gun handy, usually by the back door, to shoot at coyotes, weasels or other vermin who wondered onto the property. When my father came out of the house with the gun, my grandfather was already in his old truck waiting and they took off in pursuit. It was dark and they could see by the single head lamp of this car, which was more like a bicycle with a motor, that they had taken a wrong turn, a dead end, when leaving the property. "We got um now," said my grandfather as he pulled to the side of the rode at the intersection, cut the engine, turned off the lights and waited for their prey. As they rounded the corner my grandfather barked, "Give me the gun." In my father's excitement he smashed my grandfather in the nose with the gun as he passed it to him. Blood streamed immediately out of his broken nose. Unfazed, my grandfather pointed the single-shot 12 gauge out the window as the boys rounded the corner. When they were just feet away my grandfather pulled the trigger and shot their car at point blank range. The next day the county sheriff came out to the house and asked, "Michael, did you really shoot at those boys?" Apparently, the shot gun blast tore a hole in the back side of their car. My dad, who could imitate the deep Polish accent of his father, would always end the story by saying, "No, no, I shoot for the tire." Amazingly, this was enough of an explanation for the sheriff.

My grandpa Kania, my mother's father, had the same attitude about wasting bullets. My dad, and Uncles Rudy, Albert, and Jim told this story at least once every deer season and I never tired of it. I hunted with them even before I could carry a gun when I could only serve as a "driver" trying to move the deer out of the swamps into the open. Years before I was even born, my grandfather shot a large buck from a blind he had made out of an enormous White Pine stump that was still around during my hunting days. Because the loggers harvested the pine during the winter, the trees were cut off at the snow line leaving massive stumps once the snow melted. This stump was about 4 feet high and hollowed out, making enough room in the stump for two grown men to sit comfortably. The forest must have looked quite different here when these giants ruled the woods before the lumber barons chopped down nearly everyone of them to build Chicago and Milwaukee.

Although the story seemed to get bigger each year, the real story was that my grandfather hated to waste a bullet on a wounded animal and liked to polish them off with his knife by cutting the jugular. He shot a buck from the blind and he was so sure that it was dead that he proceeded to position himself to start gutting. He jabbed the knife into the deer's gut but it started to get up. Here is where the story occasionally gets exaggerated with some of the stories having him riding the deer around the woods. The truth seems to be that he wrestled the struggling animal back to the ground where he was eventually able to hit a critical region with his knife amid kicking hoofs and thrashing antlers.

As I rounded the corner on the gun aisle in Hoholek's store the creaky wood floor would announce my presence to Mr. Luoma, the Finnish butcher. He was always standing next to his butcher block, blood on his apron, cleaver or some oversized knife in his hand, white hat always tipped to one side.

The Finns were just one of a number of ethnic groups who arrived from the "ol country" to work in the mines, buy a farm, and start a new life. But the Finns stood out. They spent a lot of time speaking Finnish, unlike the other immigrants who banished their native tongue. This seemed to create a good deal of suspicion among the other immigrants most of whom arrived in the early 1900s. My grandparents spoke Polish to each other but mostly in the confines of their own home. My father's first language was Polish and he used it with his parents but never with us. He told us that his teachers would smack them if they spoke Polish in school. The Finns must have taken quite a beating in school because they spoke it constantly, in public, and with enthusiasm. They even had their own TV show on Channel 6 on Sunday, "Suomi Kutso." The whole show was done in Finnish and the only words I recognized were the town names like Marquette, Ishpeming, or Covington. But this seemed to be a show that was less about the local Finns and more about the relatives back in the ol' country. Beautiful Finnish scenes would flood into our living rooms accompanied by a folk song. I imagined Mr. Luoma and his wife sitting on his sofa singing along with the music.

The Finns also had a Saturday night ritual that set them apart, the sauna. Almost every Finlander had one in their back yard but I had only been in them when not in use. A sauna was simply a small building with no windows. Inside were benches and a small wood stove, altered on top to permit a layer of rocks. Each Saturday night they would light the stove and get it so hot that it glowed red, water thrown on occasionally would give a blast of heat and steam. My dad told me that he tried a sauna with some Finlander friends when he was a kid. Once the room was hot enough you stripped off your cloths and went in buck naked. When they got a good sweat going, they started to beat themselves with willow branches. It is no wonder that the school beatings didn't faze them. My dad wasn't sure what went on next because he couldn't stand the heat any longer so he got dressed and walked home. But I know how the sauna was ended. Once their bodies were red with heat and the whipping they ran out and rubbed snow on their bodies if it was winter and if there was no snow they jumped in the pond if they had one or just doused themselves in a cold bucket of water. This is, no doubt, where my grandfather got the saying, "crazy ol' Finlander."

Another area of suspicion was the Lutheran church, where the Finlanders went but not every Sunday like us Catholics. You could tell which one was the Lutheran church just by the tall untrimmed grass in the summer and un-shoveled walk in the winter. The church with the nicely trimmed yard was the Catholic Church, which we attended every Sunday with the Italians.

I learned a lot of useful information about Finlanders from my family in an indirect way. When we drove past a recently logged "forty" that was particularly tangled with tree tops and branches, my father, grandfather, or uncles would say, "damn Finlanders." They would also point out the neatly logged forties where the work was done by the Kudwas or Wolaks. "See how nice and neat that is?" I wasn't dense. Finns were messy loggers and Pols somehow cut trees down neatly.

The trouble is my room always seemed very untidy as hard as I tried to keep it neat. In my mind, it was more efficient and practical to have several changes of clothes ready at all times. No time was wasted as I could grab play, school, or church clothes right off the chair or the neat pile by my bed. Firemen used the same concept to get dressed fast when the alarm went off. And if I was especially interested in a game or toy, I liked to keep it on the floor in plain sight for my enjoyment. My mom had my dad build shelves the length of my back wall to help me get organized but I only put things on the shelves when they needed to go into deep storage. The useful, current group of toys and games covered my floor prompting my mom to remark, "I can't even walk in your room without stepping on something!" That was an exaggeration. You could walk fine in my room if you just knew where to step.

You had to pass my room on the way to the bathroom, and if my mom forgot to remind me to shut my door when we had guests over there was certain to be a comment.

"Matt, I think you got yourself a 'guldarn' Finlander," someone would inevitably say to my dad while glaring at me. I would cringe and run to close my door.

My possible Finnish descent was made all the more suspicious by Mr. Luoma's insistence that I learn Finnish every time I visited his butcher area at the back of the store. I secretly loved the lessons.

"*Matte Boyca,*" which meant "Matt's boy," he bellowed, cleaver in hand as he peered over the counter. I don't think he even knew my name but it always seemed like the highlight of his day when I walked in. He would then proceed to say something in Finnish.

"*Aldf lafdladfh ldfhaldfh, Matte Boyca.* What did I say?"

I shrugged my shoulders.

"I said, 'How is the weather today, *Matte Boyca?*' Here, repeat after me," Mr. Luoma instructed between rapid chews on his gum. He chewed it in short strokes and had the ability to make it crack every forth time. We would go over each word until I had it down, complete with the correct accent.

"Now, *Matte Boyca,* tell me all the words you know in Finnish."

I would repeat each of the dozen or so words he had taught me and he would listen intently and make small corrections.

"Now, ask how the weather is," he asked between cracks of his gum. I would give him the sentence back perfectly. He smiled showing me a missing tooth; not the front one but one of the teeth you could only see if he smiled, which was rarely.

"Ahhh, *Matte Boyca,* you make a good Finlander."

I cringed. I don't recall that he had ever been to our house and seen my room, but maybe he had heard something. It was a small town, after all.

The garden was the most beautiful display of Polish descent. Pols had weedless gardens with straight rows. Summer visitors would always be invited into the garden and even if the plants were just coming up there was much to be proud of. My sisters and I were privy to the secret of weedless gardens as we spent many painful hours on our hands and knees ridding the soil of the intrusive plants like each one was Satan himself. I hated weeding the garden. One row seemed liked hours of agony, and the day never hotter and the bugs were never worse than when you were weeding. Each minute seemed to drag on for an hour.

But I loved to weed with my dad. If there was an Olympic event in weeding he would have been an easy winner. He and I could weed the entire garden in no time flat. It also gave us time to talk. Actually, I did nearly all of the talking, my dad did most of the weeding and listening but he did not seem to mind.

One afternoon after he got home from work my dad inspected our assigned weeding for the day while I tagged along. I walked so close behind that I could smell him. I loved the way he smelled. It was a mix of sweat, pine needles, and truck exhaust fumes.

"Not bad," he said as he walked up and down the two rows and pulled out the ones we missed. "Let's see if we can finish up before dinner."

We started side by side in our rows but within seconds he was way ahead. He was the Tasmanian Devil of weeding. He used both hands and the weeds, dirt, and sweat would fly. Even when he came to an area without weeds, his thick fingers would dig into the dirt, smooth over rough spots, break up clumps, and turn over the moist soil. I suppose I could weed faster but it was hard for me to weed and talk at the same time.

"I beat Richie today in a race and he is almost three years older," I announced.

"Wow."

"I think I'm really getting fast. My legs seem to be going really fast."

"I've noticed you're a lot faster," my dad replied from within the whirlwind of weeding.

"I am just about to catch Karen," actually both of my sisters were still quite a bit faster.

"Fast is good."

"Cheetah is still a lot faster than me and anybody else in the short races but I think I could beat him in a long race. I can't believe how much faster I've gotten this summer."

"Has the weeding gotten faster too?" he paused, then winked and smiled.

Not really, I thought to myself. I had a hard time talking and weeding at the same time. I was now half done with a row and my dad was done with the rest of the garden. He came over, and in a flurry of dust and weeds my row was completed too. I just watched in total awe.

"That's it," my dad announced as he straightened up, stretched his back and surveyed our work.

I looked it over too, and it actually did look very nice and neat.

"Let's go and see what's for dinner," he announced, sniffing the air like a dog and pretending to smell something delicious.

He picked up the rake and I continued our most interesting discussion of my great speed. I sprinted to the tree and back.

"That WAS fast!" he said. I smiled.

"I bet I can even beat you," I stated boldly. My dad was the strongest man I knew. He never rolled up his sleeves or wore sleeveless shirts but he had arms like oak branches and his hands, calloused and rough, were like vice grips. When he worked you could see his back muscles ripple beneath his Sears and Roebuck's work shirt like a cougar's muscles under his skin. But I had never seen him run flat out before and I was sure I could beat him. He was a Sherman Tank, angular, strong, but slow, while I was like a rabbit, small, light and greasy fast. Plus he was older than some of the other dads and I was no doubt near the peak of my speed. "Think I can beat you?" I asked, giving him a chance to bow out with his dignity.

"Oh, I don't know," he said without much conviction.

"I'll race you. Race you back to the garage." I laid down the challenge that I was sure he would reject.

"OK," he said nonchalantly.

"Let's get Karen," I said excitingly, "she can be the starter. It's very important to have a fair start. Joey wins a lot of races but he always jumps the gun."

"I don't think we need a starter," my dad interrupted. "You just start whenever you're ready."

That seemed like a strange way to start a race. I looked up at him and he was carrying a rake. "You can put the rake down and I'll come back for it."

"That's OK, I'll just carry it."

I gave him a puzzled look. This wasn't going to be any fun. He was just going to let me win. That was little kid's stuff. "You're really going to try, aren't you?" I didn't want to race if he wasn't going to try.

"Oh sure."

"Just start anytime?" I asked.

"Whenever you're ready."

I got down in my Jesse Owens sprinter's starting position, my dad looked down at me and smiled. I gazed ahead and took off like a shot out of a rifle. I was flying. My legs were pumping like pistons in a race car and air was rushing past me filling my ears.

About halfway across the yard I could hear him. The first thing I heard was the tinkle of keys and coins in his pockets, then as he got closer it sounded like a horse pounding the ground as it rounded the bend. He was getting close but we were nearing the finish line. Out of the corner of my eye, about even with my shoulder, I could see his size 11 work boot. By the time we got to the driveway he was two enormous steps ahead of me. The finish line was the garage and he put out his massive hands to break his speed and he rushed into the wall with such force that the whole building shuddered. I scampered in right behind him and stopped without even touching the wall. He looked down at me and smiled. Then he put his head back and laughed. I did too. He rustled my hair, put his big arm around me and pulled me in close.

Of all the memories I have of my dad, this one is the most vivid and I catch myself reliving it often. It's like today routinely watching the videos of our children; they can recall the taped events like Christmas morning or school concerts because their memory gets refreshed regularly. I also think that I can recall it so clearly as it goes to the heart of the relationship between my father and me. I loved to work with him, which I continued to do through my teenage years. I didn't always like getting up at 5:00 a.m. on Saturday mornings nor did I necessarily enjoy the sometimes exhausting and often boring work. I loved to work with him because it provided opportunities to talk, moments of physical contact, and it was simply the two of us.

Like a lot of dad's, physical contact with their children usually came to a halt at puberty, especially in the U.P. The wrestling, tickling, and physical horseplay seemed to end abruptly when we were no longer "kids" anymore. This is, it seems to me, a terrible time to stop touching as you enter a gawky self-conscious time when you really could use a hug. But many kids, if they were like me, still yearned for physical contact after puberty. The type of work my dad and I did involved a lot of close physical contact, and this was the reason I could drag myself out of bed early Saturday mornings without complaint.

Most of the work we did took place on the 40 acres of land that my parents owned. My grandfather's farm was just a stone's throw away from their property and very near to where my father and his dad waited with the 12-gauge shotgun for the two boys in their three-cylinder Duryea. Half of the property was open field and the rest wooded. We were either cutting wood or tilling the fields as his farming background always called him back to working the soil. A lot of the work involved a 1950s era tractor, a red International Harvester that he kept in pristine condition. To get from the small barn to the work site, he always drove and I would stand behind him on the tractor hitch and have to wrap my arm around him to keep from bouncing off. Once we got to the site we worked side-by-side hauling rocks, planting potatoes, hoeing ridges, or carrying wood. And then there was the ride back to the barn, our clothes soaked through with sweat and covered with dirt, where I would once again take my position on the tractor, each of us feeling tired yet gratified.

Sometimes the work we did required combining our strength, and these were the moments I liked best. If a bale of hay on top needed to be adjusted or a log had to be pushed in, Dad would say, "Climb up there and fix it, I'll hold you." As I climbed the pile of logs or stack of hay bales he would grab the back of my pants with one hand while the other was put in the middle of my back to support me as I did the work. I could feel his power and the security of his grip. I knew he always had me. Sometimes I would take my time with the task or just linger a bit after I was done to enjoy the moment until I could feel his arms start to quiver from my weight.

We also talked as we worked. Not a lot, but certainly more than we talked around the house. Boys and men might be distinctively different than females as the latter seem to have little trouble conversing about their feelings without prompting or forewarning. My daughter can talk at an intimate level without much difficulty whereas my son is like a lot of boys in that they have to be engaged in an activity before they want to talk. Shooting baskets on the driveway, walking, kayaking, or just watching TV seem to be required before any discussion will start. My father and I talked as we worked. Four hours of working side by side may have only given us 10 minutes of talking but yet it seemed to make all the toil worth it.

Chapter 3

Bullies and Brawls

With my father no where near and even now in the grave, I can still feel his strong hand in the middle of my back, sometimes keeping me from falling and other times pushing me to new heights. The hand on my back was really the love I felt from both of my parents. The easiest and most natural thing a parent can do is to love their child without conditions, yet this is something that is often messed up. A parent's unconditional love is the safety net that keeps you from dropping too far should you fall, and it is the hand on your back holding you up and pushing you forward when you reach beyond your grasp. In a perfect world, mothers and fathers love their children unconditionally and they grow up to do the same with their children. But its not a perfect world today nor was it when I was growing up.

One of the remarkable attributes of my wife is being able to love the seemingly unlovable, whether it be an angry old man in a nursing home or a violent criminal. Somehow she learned that everyone has a story, and until we know their story we should not immediately turn people away or judge them just because they are different. This is similar to "cultural relativity," the core concept of anthropology and my chosen field of study. The concept basically means that there is a great diversity among people in all things like how or what they eat, how they choose people to marry, or how they deal with those who break the rules—diversity is the norm and there is not an innately right or wrong way to do things. Anthropologists seek to understand how these behaviors work relative to that particular culture and not simply judge it as right or wrong based on our culture. Many can see the value of this concept, like unconditional love, yet putting it to practice is not so easy. Much of the hatred, violence, bigotry, and war can be traced to an intolerance between people. There has been no greater intolerance in

33

our country than between whites and blacks, and race relations were a part of my childhood despite the fact that there were no black people in my town or in any of the surrounding communities.

Guess who's coming to dinner, staring Audry Hepburn and Sidney Poitier, won the 1968 Academy Award for best picture. It was a movie about an inter-racial love affair, which was something that was quite shocking in many parts of the country and especially in areas like the U.P. where there were almost no black people except in the city of Gwinn, which was home to K.I. Sawyer Air Force Base. Since closed, the base once was part of the strategic air defense, and jets armed with nuclear bombs were in the air 24 hours per day. Window rattling sonic booms and tree-top flyovers were a common occurrence in Alpha.

When I was about 16, I was hunting alone for deer behind my grandfather's farm and enjoying the wintry scene. The snow was hanging on the trees and it was so quiet that I could hear clearly the chirps of a chickadee that was a hundred yards away. It was such a wonderful, relaxing scene, one that might inspire a water-color painting, that I decided to sit on a stump in the sun and take it all in. I was day dreaming and close to dozing off when I was startled by movement just above the trees. It was a fighter jet that was flying so low that I could make out the numbers and letters on its side. The jet passed instantly and was followed by an explosion of sound so intense that all the snow resting quietly on the boughs fell to the ground, shattering the tranquility and wintry beauty. My reflexive reaction was to point my 300 Savage deer rifle to the sky for a shot. Luckily, I regained my senses before I pulled the trigger, and even if I had shot, the jet would have been miles away and far out of range. My solitary time was so completely destroyed by the violent intrusion that it took more than a half hour of walking before I felt the built up steam slowly escape through my pores. It made me feel quite helpless against the Air Force who, I suppose, considered the U.P. so underpopulated that their pilots didn't have worry as they flew over what probably looked like an endless canopy of trees.

Besides nuclear bombs, sonic booms, and startling flyovers, the base also had a lot of soldiers, bringing to the U.P. a diversity of people including African Americans. Because they were stationed at the base for 2-3 years at a time, the soldiers brought their families who got involved in the local community and schools. When I was in high school we had a football scrimmage with Gwinn, and for weeks before all we could talk about was playing against the colored kids. I'm sure the coaches were interested in working out the kinks of our offense and defense, but all I wanted to do was to tackle a black kid and get close look. The experience was anti-climatic. Although they looked and talked differently than us, they sure didn't seem much like the blacks we were seeing on TV, shouting angrily, over-turning cars, and staging protests with clenched fists in the air.

Although at first glance you wouldn't think that Alpha had much diversity, the good people of our town were still given many chances to test their tolerance. Alpha certainly had their share of eccentric people, and none more different than the Foresman's who lived in an unpainted, dingy, dark, and spooky house on First Street. Every time I passed it I walked quickly and tried to look straight ahead. When I would have the nerve to steal a glance at the house, I was certain I saw someone looking at me from behind the darkened windows. Some days I would continue my brisk walking but when my will power was low or my imagination on high, I would kick into a full sprint until I was well clear of the house. We dared each other to go there on Halloween. Many said they did but I doubted each story as I never had the courage to knock on their door. The best I could do was run through their yard, which I did once on a dare. I was so afraid that I sprinted up hill for two blocks aided by an extreme adrenaline rush. When I couldn't run anymore, I got the nerve to turn around and look back. I was up hill from the Forsman's house so I could see into their back yard, and there stood old Mr. Foresman holding an axe and looking right back at me. It was probably a coincidence, but that didn't keep me from telling and embellishing this story for years to come about being chased by an axe-wielding Mr. Foresman, and thus doing my small part in adding to their mystique.

When I got older I took on a paper route, delivering the *Iron Mountain News* to 70 or so houses in Alpha. When Pucker, the older retiring paperboy, was showing me the route, he bravely and without comment walked into the Foresman's yard, opened the door, and tossed in the paper. When he opened the door I got a strong whiff of kerosene, which they used for lighting as this was the only house in town without electricity.

"They've always been a bit odd," my dad told me. "Always keep to themselves, never go out much. I don't believe that they ever owned a car or ever got their house wired for electricity. Can you imagine?" my dad said with a smile and a laugh. My dad found them odd, humorous, and harmless while I found them eerie and dangerous.

Once per month we paperboys "collected," an arduous process that involved knocking on doors and asking for the subscription money that we kept track of with a confusing book-keeping system involving giving them small stamps from a book as a receipt. I hated the process. On a good day in the summer, you could finish the route in about an hour. Collecting added about two hours to the job as you not only knocked on each door but often engaged in small talk or heard complaints about the high cost of the paper. But collecting at the Foresman's house, even after I had been doing it for years, put a chill down my spine and kicked my overactive imagination into gear. I collected on the last Friday of each month, and the Foresman's had a routine that was in use as long as several generations of paperboys could remember. Without knocking, you walked into their house and the collection money was always neatly piled on the sink, paid always in quarters, dimes, nickels, and pennies. Sometimes Mr. or Mrs. Forseman would be sitting at the table or working at the sink when I walked in, but they wouldn't say anything or acknowledge that I was there. This routine went on unchanged until one day when I opened the door and ran right into Mr. Forseman, who grabbed me around my shoulders to keep himself from falling as I burst into his porch. I was about 15 years old at the time and much bigger than Mr. Forsman. To my surprise and relief he started laughing.

"You play football, eh?" he said, which were the first words I had ever heard him speak.

"Well, yes," I stammered.

"I read about you sometimes in the newspaper. Keep up the good work."

"OK," I squeaked.

Although I delivered papers for less than a year after this encounter it changed everything about my visits. I went into their home without the hair on the back of my neck standing up on end and I always said "hi" on collection days, which was usually returned with a nod and a smile.

But certainly the best place to see "different" people, and plenty of them, was the big city. We made an occasional family pilgrimage to Chicago to see the Field Museum or the Museum of Science and Industry, or to Milwaukee to see their zoo or catch a ball game. I loved to go to the big cities and my neck would get stiff looking up at the immense buildings, which seemed as big as mountains. But what I liked best was the chance to observe so many people.

In Alpha I knew everyone but in Chicago hundreds of people walked past and all of them strangers. But it was amazing how many times we thought we saw someone we recognized. We seemed, however, to be the only ones actually looking at the faces of other people. Everyone else walked too fast and either looked at the ground or stared blankly further down the street like there was no one else on the sidewalk. I saw far more people in two minutes than lived in our whole town.

"Don't stare," would be our mother's constant reminder but she seemed to be staring a little too. How could I not be interested? I was seeing people who looked and talked differently. The black people were especially interesting as issues about race and inequality streamed into homes through the TV news. During the 1968 Olympic Games in Mexico City, Tommie Smith and John Carlos, both black, medaled for the U.S. in the 200 meter race. To symbolize black poverty they stood without shoes on the medal podium with their heads bowed and their black-gloved fists defiantly raised during the playing of the National Anthem.

A few months earlier, on April 4th, 1968, Martin Luther King was assassinated as he walked along the balcony of the Lorraine Motel in Memphis, Tennessee.

Walter Cronkite gave the details that spring evening that went something like this.

"Ralph Abernathy cradled the dying Martin Luther King, Jr. in his arms as the other members of the King party pointed to the location of the shooter, who appears to have fired the fatal bullet from a building across the parking lot," Cronkite explained in a solemn voice.

Uncle Walter was giving us lots of bad news that spring and more was on the way. Each night the headlines did not just discuss the dying in Vietnam but rather the dying in our own streets as black people reacted violently to the killing of Martin Luther King, Jr.

"Today, President Johnson asked for calm in our cities' streets as violence erupts in our own backyards. Los Angeles, Detroit, and Chicago saw the most unrest today. So far 40 people have died, over 2,000 injured, and 21,000 people have been arrested."

We all watched in horror as our military marched into the streets. Our new color TV made the fires burning in downtown Detroit seem much closer than the 400 miles by car. Mickey Lolich, Bill Freehan, Al Kaline, Willie Horton, and the rest of the World Champion Detroit Tigers played just blocks away from the rioting and the smoke could be seen by both the players and fans. I thought the world was ending. It sure seemed that way by watching the TV. Our priest and my Baltimore catechism encouraged this idea, at least in my mind. The world was going to end and Jesus was going to return. It could be in a thousand years, it could be in a hundred years, or it could be tomorrow, we were told at the time.

What would the end of the world be like? Would angels come down from heaven and would we hear the booming voice of God? That seemed real scary. I was afraid I might pee my pants if the angels started carrying us away as we watched the bad folks burn in misery. What would St. Peter think if I peed my pants? And how could I be certain that I wouldn't be left behind? I tried to be a good boy, but who knows? What if they caught me on a bad day? I sure hoped that this wouldn't be the way the world ended and that it wouldn't end today.

Would the world explode in a big nuclear war? My parents had prepared for such an event. We had water and food stored in our basement should there be a nuclear attack, so that seemed like an unlikely way for the world to end. But maybe the end of the world starts with our burning cities? Some nights during this time I had trouble sleeping, tossing and turning, staring at the ceiling, or flipping over my pillow to rest my head on the cool side, hoping that would make me more restful. When sleep would still not come, I sometimes would get out of bed and look out the window, which had a clear view of Bear Cave Hill. If I was lucky, I might catch a glimpse of the Northern Lights, the spectacular blue and green waves of light moving like loose sails flapping in a gentle wind. Because the two windows in my room faced south and east, the best view of the lights required me to press my cheek against the cool glass.

I discovered, eventually, that the best strategy to cure my insomnia was to listen closely for the comforting sounds of my dad's heavy breathing, just across the hall. When he fell asleep he breathed slow and deep and made a sound like wind moving through the branches of a tall Norway pine. I would try to mimic the slow, deliberate sound and soon be off to sleep.

In the light of day, the dark images of the night, real or imagined, were not so scary. But TV news with burning buildings, young people throwing rocks, and police with batons and fire hoses will always be images etched in my mind. From my perspective as a young boy, it was hard to know who was the good guy and who was the bad guy. Martin Luther King, Jr. won a Nobel Peace Prize and was a champion for the black community. They had lost their champion. They had lost their leader for nonviolent change and now they had turned to violence. In my hometown it seemed much easier to know who was right or wrong.

The bullies were wrong, and everyone knew who the bullies were. They were the bad kids, the mean kids, the kids who wanted to kill you. Fighting was something that happened often in our town and school and it always involved a good kid and a bully. Bullies only fought when they knew they could win and they did most of the school yard fighting. I was the exception. I was a self-righteous brawler and I would get in fights often. I indirectly blame my teachers, parents and village priest for my fighting, combined with a world that seemed to have a tolerance for violence. I believed every word my teachers and religious leaders told me about right and wrong. "Stand up for the oppressed." "Fight for the underdog." "Defend those who cannot defend themselves." I took these statements quite literally. Children tend to believe everything their teachers, coaches and religious leaders tell them unless we have reason to believe otherwise. If your teachers, nuns and priests tell you to stand up for the weak, and we are all God's children, you absorb every word unless you hear something different at home. If teachers tell you that racism is wrong but your hear racist statements in your home, any positive effect by the teachers is voided. If the priest tells you that we must stand up for the less fortunate and weak, and your father beats you up or hits your mother then the words of the priest will bounce off instead of stick. My parents didn't do anything to contradict these words of wisdom and they became imbedded in my soul.

As a result, I became a self-righteous fighter for the weak. Somewhere along the way I must have missed the sermon about turning the other cheek or nonviolent resistance. Maybe this lesson didn't stick because of the violent world that surrounded me and the images I saw on the TV news. My attitude as the defender of all and my affinity for rough physical contact and an above average temper, created lots of opportunities for violence. I was on a mission. I never meant to get into fights, but when I would get picked on, or someone else would get picked on I would see red. Something would snap and suddenly I was Ray Nitschke chasing down a ball carrier. Other kids sulked away from the bullies but I stepped in and usually got beat up. The only reward was getting a few good licks in.

Mr. Marinello, our school principal, could always tell when a fight broke out in the school yard. With one eye always on the children during recess, he would work in his third story office that faced the playground. Cheers and shouting would erupt and phrases like, "fight!" "Kill'um," or "punch him" could be easily heard from his third floor office. He would watch for a moment from his window to determine what action to take. He was born and raised in Alpha so he understood bullies. Many of the bullies today were the kids of the bullies when he was in school. We could often see him in the window. He was the only man in Alpha who wore a tie every day. He was once a good basketball player as there was a picture of him and the state championship team on the wall of the hallway that led into our gym. He had gained some weight since highschool but the stern, unsmiling face I saw on the basketball photos was the one he still wore.

Most of the fights were wrestling matches but I so often found myself outmatched that I would quickly resort to punching. I had a pair of leather mittens (choppers) that even looked like boxing gloves and they would save my fists from the sting of a blow. Despite my efforts to escalate the violence in my favor I was usually over-powered by a bigger, stronger opponent. Once a fight started there was an unwritten rule, which I almost always violated, that prohibited others from getting involved. My friends would never jump in either because they believed in the notion of a fair fight or they were just afraid. If my sister Karen was nearby she might jump in to my rescue. It gave me great pride to see her dive into the pile, wild hair flying, neck vein bulging, risking her reputation to save her little brother. I always told her not to do it because I would get teased later for needing my sister, a girl, to help me, but I usually hoped she would appear when I was pinned and my face was getting ground into the icy playground.

Years later when I was a young adult, Mr. Marinello told me that if a good kid was beating up a bully he would watch for a while and maybe even take a bite or two from his lunchtime sandwich before walking casually down the stairs to the playground to break up the fight. If a bully was beating up a good kid he would disappear quickly from the window and take the stairs two or three steps at a time. When I was fighting, he reminded me, he would usually have to run down the stairs.

During my brawling days, my dad and I bumped into Mr. Marinello and he told my dad, "Jimmy here has a temper like an Irishman. He is going to get himself killed picking fights with the big kids." I looked down at my shoes but I could feel both pair of eyes staring down at me. On the ride home my dad and I sat in silence for most of the way and I hoped, without success, that we would make it all the way home and not talk about my fighting at school.

"It's OK to walk away from a bully, you know," my dad said, breaking the silence. "If someone attacks, you can defend yourself but most of these fights I think you can avoid."

I couldn't see Ray Nitschke or my dad walking away from a bully.

"When I was a kid I learned to run fast trying to get away from the bullies," my dad continued.

In my mind, it was unlikely that my dad ever ran from a bully. This seemed like the kind of thing parents say just to make a point. Maybe the kids were different back then, I thought. But these few words from my principal and my dad made me think. I vowed to try and stay away from fighting.

It worked for a while but eventually, in a world full of bullies, more conflict was inevitable. One morning as we waited for the school bell to ring, a group of older kids approached us. Some of them were bullies while the others were just hanging out with them, but everyone knew that this was a dangerous gang. They walked toward our little group like wolves sizing up the sheep herd, and everyone tensed up. It didn't take them long to live up to their reputation, as one of them grabbed a hat and start tossing it around. Usually they enjoyed grabbing some little girl's hat so they could make her cry. The group of bullies would toss it around, take turns putting it on their greasy heads or pretending to wipe their butt with it. This was exactly the type of bully behavior that made my blood boil and would set me off. I would say something like, "Knock it off you assholes!" The words would be out of my mouth before I knew what I was saying. I could feel the rage start in the pit of my stomach then move quickly up through my chest, down my arms, and up the back of my neck. The air temperature could be below freezing but I could feel my face suddenly glow fire-red. This is the way most of my fights started.

"You're dead," they would say and then move in for the kill. Someone grabbed my hat and started tossing it around as they suddenly lost interest in the little girl's hat.

"Look here, now we have little baby Jimmy's hat, what's he going to do about it?"

This was ordinarily the time when I would rush in, get a few hits in before getting pummeled by the thugs. But Mr. Marinello's words to my dad, "Jimmy here has a temper like an Irishman," and my dad's later words, "You can run away from bullies," made me hesitate. I stood there, paralyzed. They sensed my indecision.

"What's the matter baby Jimmy, are you chicken? Don't you want your hat back?" They said as they clucked with glee.

I just stood there and watched my hat being tossed around. Other kids joined in too. Even the little girl whose hat they had initially stolen caught my hat once and tossed it while joining in the laughter. The school bell rang, saving me from further humiliation. One of the bullies caught the hat last, looked at me with a sneer and tossed it high in the tree. I turned and went toward the front door.

I walked to my home room, but I was burning with rage and humiliation. The no-fight policy seemed so stupid. How were these bullies ever going to learn if we all stood back and watched? The Bible verse about turning the other cheek may have worked thousands of years ago but today, in Alpha, it seemed impractical and dangerous. In my fiery rage I plotted ways to get back at the bullies. Maybe I could get his lunch bag and fill it with dog shit. Another good one would be to secretly get his hat and put it in the school toilet.

As I thought of various pay-backs my rage slowly escaped. My jaw unclenched, my neck and shoulders dropped, my face no longer had the red glow of a boxer, and my mind was now thinking rationally. This was the time after a fight when I would start to feel the places where I had been hit; the lumps on my head, sore ribs, the salty taste of blood, or a fat lip. The only benefit I could see from the walk-away policy was the lack of injuries, and this seemed to be a small prize compared to the humiliation I felt from the bullies and even the spectators who urged me on but then thought of me as a wimp when I backed down. I would have much preferred the visible battle scars.

That night as Walter Cronkite announced the news, I got the chance during a commercial to tell my dad about the day's events. I expected him to say that I should have charged the bullies after he took my hat. But instead he replied, "Seems like you did exactly the right thing." I was perplexed.

"You mean I should just stand back and take it?" I said in dismay.

"You handled it just right," is all my dad would tell me.

"But I've got to get him back," I said and then revealed some of my secret plans for revenge.

"The bullies probably get beat up by their ol' man every day," dad replied. "Anything you do to them will not even get close to that. Forget about it. Stay away from those kids if you can," my dad suggested. He made it sound so easy. How could I "stay away" from kids I saw every day? These bullies were like a pack of wolves and very good at what they did. If they sensed that I was weak, they would pounce at every opportunity. Despite my reservations, I vowed to give nonviolence another try.

I got into a few more fights over the years, but overall the plan seemed to be working. It also helped that I grew in size and strength, which made it less likely the bullies would pick on me as they always seem to prefer preying on the younger and weaker. The school in Alpha closed down soon thereafter, yet another sign of our slowly dying town since the closing of the mine. Our school district consolidated with Crystal Falls, located just five miles away. New school, new kids, and plenty of potential conflict. But guided by my parents and teachers, my new attitude seemed to be working. I was no longer so quick to turn to violence, and was much better at keeping my hot temper in check. I still did, however, maintain the belief that if I was attacked and provoked there was just cause for immediate and violent reaction. This policy, however, was tested and came into question one morning on the playground.

The details of the event escape me but I do recall that it started during our ongoing game of marbles, which was our winter obsession. We played a simple game, more like golf than marbles. With the heel of our boot, we dug a hole in the hard-packed playground snow and then paced off several yards. Each player picked a marble from their collection. The "biggies" and the "steelies" worked best, but you used these prizes with caution as the winner of the game kept the other player's marble. The object of the game was to get your marble into the hole first. A good player would know how conditions affected the way the marble rolled.

I was involved in a match and one of us was about to shoot when a young kid cried out and landed on his back with a dull thud right in the middle of our game. He was kind of annoying but he was only a 2nd grader and Tom, the kid who pushed him down was in 4th grade and twice his size. Tom was a quiet kid and had never been in any trouble, so I asked him, "What's the matter with you?" I expected him to say that the kid was being a turd and that he deserved the vicious push but instead he took an unexpected round-house swing at me. I could easily have ducked such a swing but this one caught me by surprise and found its mark right around my left ear. When you take a direct hit like this it really hurts. In the movies the guys paste each other time after time, but in real life when you get smacked like that your whole head explodes in pain. As I reeled backwards my hearing shut off temporarily and the sounds of the playground were reduced to a muffled roar. I fell backwards on the ground. I expected him to jump me at any moment but knew I was defenseless trying to shake off the blow. Quickly the pain and the cobwebs were overtaken by a rush of anger and power.

Engulfed in rage, I jumped up and zeroed in on Tom. I charged him and scored a direct right to his head that rocked him back. I moved in and scored two more easy hits. The sound of my chopper-covered fists hitting his face made a sickening noise like hitting an apple with a baseball bat. Sounds and scenes that would normally be quite disturbing could be easily ignored in a fight. I always felt wonderfully alive in a fight. The rush of adrenaline made me feel omnipotent, and even if I was getting beat up I wanted to continue like an over-matched boxer in a prize fight pleading with his manager to let the fight go on.

On this day, however, something seemed wrong. Tom really wasn't fighting back. For the last punched I grabbed his collar and belted him right in the mouth. He fell to the ground and immediately started to cry.

"See what happens when you pick on someone your own size!" I taunted. He was curled up like a baby on the playground snow, a trickle of blood running down his chin from his split lip. I had never seen anyone act like this after a fight. I was confused and immediately felt a bit guilty.

The bell rang ending recess and we headed for the door. The fight happened so fast that it seemed no one but us had seen it. I looked back at the playground as I went in the door and I could see Tom's coat sticking out from behind a tree.

When we got to our room and sat down, Mr. Hronkin got us started on our work. After a few minutes, another 4th grade teacher poked her head in the door and asked Mr. Hronkin to step into the hall. I sat there tense, waiting to be called out too, but he came back into the room and casually resumed the lesson.

Morning passed slowly and the bell finally rang, announcing lunch and everyone got up excitedly. I got in line last and walked out the door. Mr. Hronkin was standing in the hall looking grim. I looked at the ground. As I passed him he put his hand on my shoulder.

"Right after you eat your lunch come back up here," Mr. Hronkin said. "I want to talk to you."

Lunch was always one of my favorite times, but I couldn't eat a thing. I sat, playing with my food, wasting time trying to avoid my return to the classroom. The lunch room was always so exciting, but today I could only watch. The talking, laughing, and screaming were so loud that you had to shout to be heard. It felt awfully strange not to be engaged in the fun, to watch my friends telling jokes and doing food tricks and not be involved. It was great fun to see someone blow jello out of their nose or mix their food with their milk to make mush and drink it through a straw. Sometimes I laughed so hard at lunch that my stomach would ache. Today I just watched in silence and no one seemed to notice.

My legs felt like lead as I slowly walked up the two flights of stairs. Usually I took the stairs two or three at a time and my feet seemed like they were carried by butterflies, but today I had to use the hand rail for assistance.

The 3rd floor was quiet and I could hear the sounds of recess below. I walked toward my room, the squeaky wood floor announcing my arrival.

Mr. Hronkin was at his desk. He was young and my first man teacher. He always stood out when all the grade school teachers were standing in the hall. Most of the other teachers looked and dressed like my grandmother, but he was well over 6 feet tall, slim, but powerfully built. Rumor had it that he was once a great basketball player. We all loved him. The girls had a crush on him but the guys loved having their first man teacher. He told great stories that we could relate to. In math he would use baseball or football examples, and after deer season he spent almost an hour telling us the story of how he shot his nice eight point buck. He also had lots of practical advice that you never received from a female teacher. At recess he would often play basketball or baseball with us and give us useful tips.

Upon entering the room, he told me that he knew what happened at morning recess and that Tom's mother had come to pick him up. I cringed, thinking that he was seriously injured. "Is he hurt?" I inquired. Mr. Hronkin explained that he wasn't really physically hurt but he was hurt in another way. Tom's father died and this was his first time back in school since the funeral. All the blood drained out of me and I felt as if I was about to cry. I couldn't imagine, at least at the time, what it would be like to lose my father.

Mr. Hronkin stopped short. My eyes started to well up with tears. I thought what it would be like for my dad to die. I would be lost. Mr. Hronkin came closer and put his arm on my shoulder as I hung my head in shame. He tried to console me. "You didn't know. He punched you first."

These words did little to assuage my guilt. I should have realized that something was wrong. He was no bully. And I certainly shouldn't have slugged him those last times as he wasn't really fighting back. I should have stopped. I should have known.

"Do me a favor. Tom is going to need all the friends he can get. Try to hang around with him a little bit when he comes back to school."

"Sure," I said.

I suppose I can now relate to Tom in a new and deeper way than I could at that time. Losing your dad at any time is difficult, but it must be much harder when you are a young boy.

Less than two weeks after my dad's funeral, my family and I were back home in Illinois and, unbelievably, life was continuing. My friend Bob called and asked me if I would like to join him, Rodger and Galen for a beer. We are all about the same age and had many similar interests, but what I learned that day was that we were also bound together by the fact that our fathers had all died. "Come on, have a drink with us," Bob said sensing my hesitancy, "it will do you some good." I really didn't want to go to some smoky, noisy bar. I hadn't spent enough time with my wife and kids, my back ached, and I still felt emotionally raw. Twelve days previous my Dad had died and I'd been on an emotional roller coaster. I really didn't feel ready to talk but Bob was insistent so I reluctantly accepted his invitation.

We met at a bar that was a converted fire station. We sat outside and ordered dark beer. I knew that Bob's father died when Bob was a still a child and we had talked about his dad many times, but I didn't realize until we sat down that Rodger and Galen had lost their fathers as well. Galen's father had a stroke while driving a tractor six year's earlier. Rodger was in college when he received the word from his brother that his father had died. What a morbid group, I thought as I drank half the glass of beer in three large gulps feeling the need for a little alcohol induced numbness. A fraternity, of sorts, united by our dead fathers. I had known each of these guys for years but as we greeted each other and they offered their condolences I peered into their eyes and noticed a sadness I had not noticed before. I'd known these guys but didn't know of their secret society. A society with the cruelest of initiations, the death of your own father.

Bob, a college voice instructor and the organizer of a local theater group, had talked of his father often over the years. He died when Bob was eight. So many missed years. "I think about him every day," Bob told me one day several years ago. He thought about him everyday, yet he had just a handful of childhood memories. How many times had he played those memories over in his head? How could I really mourn? Me, with a trunk full of happy memories that could easily keep me occupied for days. What would it have been like to lose my father when I was eight. At eight I was at the height of my father worshiping and obser- vation period. I used to beg to go to work with my father during the summer months. "You'd be bored," he would tell me. Bored! A whole eight hours to observe my favorite subject; to watch the way he moved his hands, tucked in his shirt, and adjusted his cap. I observed him like an anthropologist studies an iso- lated tribe and I mimicked his every move. I ate like him, belched like him, and practiced the way he walked. Yes, eight years old would have been a bad time to lose my father, but still I would have a clear picture of him. Some of my earliest memories are the sharpest.

Rodger was a college student when his dad died suddenly. "I was immature then, and really didn't know how to deal with it," Rodger told us. "I have a lot of good memories of my father but I do regret that he never met my kids and they never got to know their grandfather." How could I be sad? My kids were his youngest grand kids and they knew him like a second father.

But what if my Dad died when I was 20 years old? This was the time when I was the smartest person in the world. My parents, on the other hand, seemed quite slow and I took every opportunity to let them know how brilliant I was. "You are quite smart," is what my parents would tell me. Now I'm reminded of Mark Twain's line that when he was younger his parents were perfectly stupid but now that he was older he was surprised to see how much smarter they had become.

My father retired when I was in college and he decided to build a log cabin, from scratch. He cut the logs, peeled them, let them dry, notched them and set them in place. I helped him a great deal during that summer but only as the assistant. He was the brains and I was the college boy with the strong back. He had never built a log cabin before but that didn't hold him back.

When I was still in high school, my dad felt that I should have a few more carpentry skills and my mother saw an ad in the paper that said that someone needed a small house remove from their property. The only reward was the salvaged lumber. So I spent a summer tearing down the building board by board. The plan was to use the material to build a storage shed, a miniature of the big red barns found in our area. I was given instructions in the morning, and slowly built the storage shed that still stands in my parent's yard. If my father died when I was 20 I would still have these memories, but I would have not gotten a chance to see him "get smarter."

Galen's father died at a ripe old age, but he could retrieve far fewer warm memories of his childhood because, it seemed, he wasn't too close to his father. Certainly, this would be the far greatest tragedy. How could I complain? There I sat with a heart full of memories of the unconditional love my parents had for me.

One small example of that support occurred during a high school football game. A requirement to playing high school football in the Upper Peninsula of Michigan is the ability to endure bad weather. But one Saturday afternoon during an away game against the Hancock Bulldogs, the weather was especially miserable. It was a hard-driving sleet/snow/ice storm blowing in from frigid Lake Superior. It was the 4th quarter and we were way ahead. Out of the corner of my eye I saw movement in what I presumed and expected to be empty bleachers. As I stood ankle deep in icy-slush and squinted through the sleet, I recognized the two forms as my mom and dad. I suddenly felt warm.

As the 3rd glass of beer was served we talked about how each of our fathers had died. I hadn't talked to anybody but family about the days leading up to my Dad's death because the sounds, smells, and the images were still painfully fresh in my mind. With the encouragement of my friends, I retold this tale with great difficulty. My upbringing was screaming at me to just nod and tell them I'd rather not talk about it, but it was their honest stories that inspired me to go on. As members of the dead father's society they knew how important it was for me to talk. So I told them the story, having to stop several times to gather myself, and felt remarkably good afterward.

Being stoic and tight-lipped about ones's feelings may be an adaptive trait for the first immigrants of the U.P., who had to saw logs all day with broken fingers, crawl down a dangerous mine shaft where someone is maimed or killed every month, or go to work the day after your infant child has died. It is, however, a maladaptive trait in my world. My father was certainly more expressive than his father, and maybe my father's final lesson to me, as seen through the eyes of my friends that night, was to be more open and expressive. There is a wonderful freedom that comes with self expression. I am still not terribly comfortable with it or very good at analyzing or even exploring my inner thoughts and feelings, but I am delighted to see that it comes much easier to our son.

Chapter 4

Buried Alive

Our son Matt came home from high school and announced that recruiters for the Illinois National Guard taught all the Physical Education classes that day. As he walked into class and realized what was going on, he thought about skipping. He asked a friend if he wanted to skip but couldn't get him or anyone else to ditch class. It's hard to go against authority alone so he attended class. The war in Iraq during the spring of 2006 was very unpopular and the recruiters were having a hard time meeting their quotas, so somehow they convinced our school's administration to let three buff and handsome recruiters, each smartly dressed in their uniforms, teach gym classes. The girls swooned and the boys noticed. They used the first half of the class to conduct team building exercises and the second half was a hard-sell recruiting pitch. If they signed up now they would be eligible to get a $20,000 signing bonus, "Just like Mark Prior gets," a star pitcher for the Chicago Cubs. Plus you would have to work just one weekend a month, according to the recruiters.

"If we joined, would we have to go to Iraq?" a student asked. "Unlikely," was their reply. I did some checking on these facts, which could be easily obtained by going to the Illinois National Guard web site where they post deployments, and within the last 30 previous days two Illinois National Guard units had been deployed to Iraq for 12 month stays. One of the deployed units was right from our town.

My wife and I sat silently stunned as our son told us of the day's events. Just three years earlier we had taken the kids to an anti-war rally at the old court house, now the McLean County Museum of History. Abe Lincoln once practiced law at this site and he gave his famous "Lost Speech" just around the corner. Now old Abe sits immortalized in bronze on a bench that invites you to sit next to him for a chat. What would Abe think about the war and the signs being waved in the air, "No Blood for Oil," "Unconstitutional, Immoral, Illegal?" I don't think he would have been disappointed to see us all there.

I had suggested that we not take Matt and Sadie to the protest because most people in our conservative town were supportive of the war. But Becky said that it would be good for the kids to see us stand up for what we believed. I wondered if it might be dangerous or at least frightening for them. It was such a small group of protesters and the steamroller for war seemed so big. As we walked around the plaza a few people yelled insults from their cars and a couple people showed us their middle finger. This upset me some but our kids seem unfazed.

Because we were so against the war in the first place, we were quite enraged to hear that our son's school was permitting the military to teach classes and to engage in their hard-sell recruiting as part of a required course. My wife and I immediately wrote a letter to the principal as did several other parents and the principal replied in a way that suggested that such a thing would not happen again.

It is both interesting and disturbing that military recruiters use to their advantage a strategy that is quite attractive to young men. They are interested in recruiting women as well, but it seems like they rely upon age-old techniques that are at the heart of male bonding. Fathers and sons, and males in general, seem to bond wordlessly in work, competitive sports, and war. There is something that attracts boys to join a team, working together toward a common goal, and, in fact, learning to love one another. The best football teams and the top-notch military units are composed of men willing to sacrifice themselves for the good of the group. There is no greater act of love than sacrificing yourself for a friend, and the military is successful at putting together groups of men and women who are willing to put themselves at risk for each other and the group. Military recruiters know this all too well and they play to the need for young men to competitively bond and belong. In my grandfather's time, however, it was the mining companies who used this same tactic to their great advantage.

My great grandfather was a horse ranch foreman in southern Poland, but was at the time Galacia, Austria. During his lifetime, Poland didn't even exist and their land was divided between Russia, Germany, and Austria. During the 18th and 19th centuries few places on earth had more battles and more farmers conscripted into one army or the other. While Poland was controlled by three outside powers there were several patriotic movements but each attempt at liberation and independence was met with more oppression. Military leaders at the time didn't need to bond units into a family as is done today, they literally filled their units with family. Interrelated men from small towns were conscripted into service as the military knew then too that you are a better soldier if the person crouching next to you in the fox hole is your brother, father, uncle, or cousin.

My great grandfather was right to encourage my grandfather to leave Galacia, Austria when he did as their homeland became the principle battlefield for WWI, and Poles were drafted into three separate militaries: Austrian, Russian, and German. Like most immigrants during the early 20th century, the Poles came to the U.S. for economic opportunity, but they also came to escape war and tyranny. In an area no larger than the state of New Mexico, Poles were forced to fight and kill one another. But my grandfather left one type of conscription for another as he, along with millions of other immigrants, were placed into a number of dangerous industries that also used familial relationships to their benefit.

My grandfather departed for the U.S. in 1907 from Bremen, Germany aboard the *Main*, and was processed through Ellis Island. The immigration papers state that he had just $6.00 to pay toward the $50.00 immigration entry fee, but they still let him in. Like the immigrants today from Latin America, it wasn't hard to find a job. In my grandfather's case, mining company recruiters hungry for labor converged on New York to entice the men to work in the iron mines. He moved to the U.P., followed by other family, and immediately started working in the mines to earn enough money to fulfill his dream of buying land and starting his own farm.

My grandfather worked in several local mines but his mining career came to an abrupt end when he was buried alive in a cave-in at the Book Mine, the last of the Alpha mines that closed just afer I was born. The mine shaft tower that lowered the miners deep into the earth was visible if you climbed the large elm tree in the field next to our house. One summer, years after the mine closed, a friend and I crawled under the fence and past the "No Trespassing" and "Danger: Caving Ground" signs to get a better look. It was like a ghost town. Grass was growing up around the tires of the old trucks that hadn't been moved in years. We went because someone told us that there were piles of "steelies," which were the stainless steel balls in great demand for our winter marble games. However, we didn't stay long enough to find any because we were spooked by the place.

"It's just the wind," I said unconvincingly as loose boards creaked and slammed on the ghostly buildings. A slow, high pitched, metal on rusty metal grinding sound coming from the shaft tower was enough for me, and we both decided it was time to go. We turned and started to walk for the hole under the fence. We walked faster with each step but a loud bang behind us put us into a full-speed run. We didn't look back until we were under the fence and in the safety of the woods.

The story of the Book Mine cave-in was well known in my family. The men worked round the clock in 12 hour shifts and many of the best jobs were composed of small teams, usually family-based. My grandfather's team, which included his brother, was to build timber supports in the tunnels as the miners blasted holes following the veins of the precious iron ore deep under ground. Working hunched over in the five foot high tunnels lit only with their helmet lamps and the single lantern hung on the wall, they erected huge pine timbers to support the roof. The most dangerous job was testing the stability of the tunnel roof and removing the loose rock, which they did by tapping and probing with a metal bar. It was my grandfather's turn to knock away the rock, which he was doing about 20 feet down the tunnel from his brother. Without warning the narrow tunnel collapsed burying him beneath tons of rock. He was pulled out hours later, unconscious, badly broken, and near dead.

The exact details are not known but I imagine that they took him to the nearest hospital five miles down a rough dirt road and my grandmother and her sister followed. They no doubt heard the cave-in whistle and came to the mine with the other wives and huddled around the entrance waiting to see if it was their night to become a widow. My grandfather's brother, who dug him from his near grave, was covered with red iron ore dirt and dust leaving no distinction between his bare skin and clothes.

When the trucks arrived at the quiet hospital they called for the doctor who lived across the street. He examined my grandfather's body through his dirt encrusted clothes and could feel a shattered pelvis, crushed ribs, and a broken leg. His shallow breathing and his weak pulse were telltale signs of imminent death. The doctor told my grandmother that death was near so his final orders to the nurse were to leave my grandfather alone, without even bothering to clean him up and remove his dirty clothes. In the words of my grandfather, years later, "God damn doctor left me for dead. They didn't even open a bed for me. I wasn't even worth a change of sheets."

The next morning the doctor no doubt expected to see the undertaker's wagon at the hospital's door, but instead found my grandfather conscious, alert, and pissed off. I only wish I could have been there when the doctor came through the door and encountered my grandfather's wrath. He had a wonderful, colorful way of cussing in a mix of Polish and English. A stuck bolt or an engine that wouldn't start would bring on angry, guttural words that were spoken in a rhythmical almost poetic way. These were well rehearsed outbursts that could be varied slightly depending on the situation. My personal favorite was the way he would say "son-of-a-bitch," which could have a wide range of uses. Sometimes it could simply mean "wow," but mostly it was directed at someone or something to show various levels of frustration or anger. The more serious the offense the greater numbers of "son-of-a's" that would be repeated. I can only imagine the doctor heard something like this, "You son-of-a, son-of-a, son-of-a, son-of a, bitch."

These long cuss-filled diatribes would sound like he was starting his old truck, which after a few cranks would finally fire and roar to life.

I've always had a hard time understanding why a doctor would be so cruel as to leave my grandfather on top of a bed, in his dirty clothes without so much as an attempt to save his life. Had he and the medical staff been instructed by the mining companies, who had to pay for the medical care, not to go through any heroic measures to save a miner? The mining companies, who were ultimately responsible for building hospitals, schools, and other public service facilities, had tremendous power in the small towns. Death and injury in the mines were common and there was a steady stream of new immigrants willing to take their places in these dangerous jobs. Or it could be that the behavior of the doctor was based on ethnic bigotry that traced all the way back to the "old country." Maybe the doctor was of German, Austrian, or Russian descent and he could recognize the southern Polish dialect of my grandmother, which stirred in him ethnic hatred that went back generations. Or maybe it was religious bigotry as Catholics of the early 20th century could be included on the list with African Americans and Jews in terms of discrimination by the ruling class. All of these reasons are certainly possible and seem to be in line with the conclusion that my grandfather reached, but it also seems possible that leaving my grandfather undisturbed at his moment of death could have been an act of mercy. Undressing a man with a shattered pelvis would have caused even more extreme pain, so maybe the doctor's decision was an act of compassion to let the broken miner die in peace. Only the doctor will ever know, but there is some joy, at least, in knowing that if his intentions were less than noble he had to endure the wrath of grandfather.

He recovered fully after spending much of the summer in a body cast that kept his hips and both legs immobilized. But with a pair of crutches he was able to get around and even hurdle a fence chasing down an escaped cow. Ironically, the accident that almost killed him may have saved his life because he never returned to the mines. His brother, however, who pulled him from the cave-in, kept working in the mine and died at a young age of "miner's consumption," which is a form of silicosis, a fatal pulmonary dust disease that afflicts anyone who works under dusty conditions without proper ventilation. The red hematite dust that covered their faces and bodies at the end of each work day also lodged in their lungs that caused them problems sometimes years later.

The grandfather I knew was less ornery and very different than the man depicted in the stories of my father, uncles and aunts. To me he was just my friendly old grandpa. His hair was completely white and thin and he moved very slow. It would take him 20 minutes to walk to church or the store, a distance I could cover in 5 to 10 minutes. The dentist had pulled most of his teeth before I was born, but he rarely used the ill-fitted dentures. Remarkably he managed to chew everything with just the few remaining teeth. His eyes were bad enough that he used a magnifying glass to read his mail and other documents, mostly letters and Polish language magazines that he kept stacked on the dining room table. He kept his reading glasses in a drawer next to his false teeth. Today, the only remnant of being buried alive were the tiny steps he took as arthritis had invaded the areas broken under the weight of the rocks. But a series of other mishaps later in life also contributed to his reduced pace.

When his eyesight was failing the sheriff took his driver's license away after several near misses. Because his mail box was a half mile from the house, he took his farm tractor to pick up the daily mail. This trip required him to cross US 2, the busiest highway in the U.P.. One afternoon he was crossing the highway and pulled out in front of a car, which slammed into the side of the tractor. He was thrown from the vehicle and he "broke his back," which required him to stay off the tractor for a while. Soon after he recovered he decided to burn some brush near the edge of an open field. He seemed to love fire as there was often a smoldering pile somewhere on his property. One windy afternoon, however, the brush pile fire got away and started to burn the field and threaten buildings. He got on his small John Deere bulldozer and was able to control the blaze but not before the bulldozer seat caught on fire giving him second and third degree burns up his back. Despite this mishap, he still maintained a certain fascination and carelessness with fire.

He and my dad decided to burn a 20 acre field to promote the growth of hay, and my dad got the necessary fire permits from the DNR who also supplied us with hand-held pump sprayers to control the fire at its borders. My father gave me a spray can and one job; follow my grandfather who insisted upon helping out with the burn. "Just put out the fires the ol' man starts," my dad instructed. My father started the fire on the west side of the field to use the prevailing winds and the fire quickly took off. My grandfather, however, wasn't satisfied with the extent of the burn, which he wanted to extend further into the woods, so he walked about lighting and tossing matches. My father could see us from afar and he pointed and waved his hands to remind me to put out his fires. Trying to be as discrete as possible, I proceeded to use the pump can to put out all of the small fires he started without letting him notice. After using up most of a book of matches, he turned around to find that none of his fires had started. After a string of cuss words he retraced his steps flicking matches as he walked. He finally used up all his matches while I still had plenty of water. I looked at my dad across the field and he gave me a thumbs up.

He took no medicine for any of his ailments from the "God damn doctors" but he was clearly stiff and in pain. Finally, a doctor, no doubt frustrated with his patient, prescribed that he take one or maybe two shots of brandy before bed or whenever the pain was too bad. This was a prescription that my grandfather could understand and it kept him quite mobile. I loved to watch him take his medicine. He would pour it into a shot glass and make it so full that the brandy was actually slightly higher than the edge of the glass. He would pick it up carefully trying not to spill a drop and then when it finally hit his lower lip he would throw it back with gusto. He would then shake his head and start to laugh and wipe the tears from his eyes with the back of his sleeve.

My grandfather moved into Alpha after my grandmother died and the farm got to be too much for him to run, and we would often get calls from his neighbor, Olga, reporting on his actions. "He's way up on the ladder chopping with an axe!" My dad and I went to investigate and sure enough he was up a ladder leaning over a little too far wacking at the buildup of ice with as much strength as his 80 year old body could muster. "What if you fall?" my dad asked.

"Then I'll get up," he said with a little disgust at the silliness of the question.

It is remarkable to me how much my grandfather and the men who went down into the mines are like soldiers on a battlefield. Like in war, each time men entered the mine they knew that they might not come out. But because they were doing the work with family and friends, they knew that they would not be abandoned in the mine should something happen. When my grandfather was buried in the cave-in, all miners came to the surface except his brother and family who stayed to dig him out. One could say that my grandfather and these other men did this work voluntarily; it was their choice to work in the mines. This conclusion is not entirely accurate and does not reflect the complexity of their situation. Given the choices that life gave them, what options did they have? Their homeland was a battlefield and they were destined to be conscripted into one army or the other to fight against their people. Compared to that fate, the mines and its dangers and at least the hope for economic advancement was a choice that was easily made.

A similar type choice befalls many of our intercity poor and the rural youth who live in places like the U.P. today, which is economically depressed. Our military is filled with these youths who see it as the only way to get a college education and improve their lives. When I travel back to the U.P. I am shocked by the number of young men and women from the area who are serving in the military and most of them today in Iraq or Afghanistan. Like the miners of my grandfather's generation, they are willing to risk their lives, not for some greater good but rather to improve their lot in life. What kid from an economically depressed area can turn down a $20,000.00 signing bonus and a college education if they live through the experience? What immigrant miner could turn down a paying job in the mines to feed his family and to possibly save few a dollars to eventually buy a piece of land?

I suppose it is ironic that my grandfather and his brothers escaped the battle-fields of Europe and being drawn into WWI just to have their own sons return to Europe to fight the same tyrants. My father and three of his brothers served in WWII. My father's uniform was hanging in our attic and his pile of medals were in my mother's jewelry box. And as a young boy I was completely captivated by his war and I pestered him about it constantly.

"What are these medals for?" I asked him one afternoon. They were thin flat bars striped with different colors.

"These are battle stars for Normandy, Northern France, and Rhineland, this is a good conduct medal, and I think this one is the European theater medal, and," he paused turning over a couple of medals in his hand, "gee I don't remember what these are for."

"What did you do in the war?"

"I was a buck Sargent, in a heavy artillery division, in the 3rd Army, General Patton's army."

"Did you ever meet Patton?" I asked excitedly.

"No," he laughed and smiled. "I don't think I was ever too close to Patton."

"What was it really like in the war?" I asked. For all the times I asked him he had only given me small glimpses of the war, and he usually retold the same stories. None of the blood and guts that I was after but I always listened with keen interest.

"The first action I ever saw was the invasion of Normandy. My outfit was with the artillery, we shot a 90 mm anti-aircraft gun and also carried a 50 caliber machine gun. I was the Sargent in charge of the gun-crew, the 16 men who shot and defended the big gun. We marched all the way across France. We were either fighting or moving forward the whole summer and fall, sometimes moving ahead so fast that we would run out of fuel or the men would run out of water."

"We came to some poor little bombed out village and my men were so thirsty that they were getting crazed. I took two men and we start going into the houses and little shops looking for water. We could walk right through the holes in the walls made by our guns. But there were no people. I always wondered what happened to the people. The private with me came across an old wine cellar, and before I could stop him he was yelling that he found something to drink. My guys came running in like mad dogs, broke the tops off the bottles and guzzled the wine like it was water. I yelled at them to stop but they were crazy with thirst. That lasted a minute or two, and then they started to puke. Everyone of the them. It was disgusting. We're all crammed in this little cellar and barfing up red wine. I'm getting a little crazy, trying to get these 16 guys out of the cellar and their filth, dragging them by their collars. They're all laying there moaning in the back alley, and I'm trying to think how I am going to get my crew back on their feet, when this one guy in our group, the comical one, sat up with red barf all over the front of his coat and says something like, 'Not a bad vintage, though I prefer the 1940 Cabernet. Doesn't have such a God damn aftertaste.' I start laughing and they all start cracking up. What a bunch of characters they was. To this day I don't like to drink wine," he finished with a wink.

"What kind of gun did you shoot," I asked.

"My group carried a machine gun, which we all could shoot, but I carried and mostly shot the M1. That was a great gun. It could shoot as fast as you could pull the trigger."

"Did you bring home any Nazi guns or knives or anything?" I asked. At other houses in Alpha there was some cool Nazi stuff, like lugers, knives, and even a helmet, which we always took turns trying on.

"Everyone had some stuff like that, but I was injured so they just shipped me out with the clothes on my back," he replied dryly. "I fell down a well in the middle of the night and tore up my knee. I don't have any souvenirs, but I've got three remembrances. I've got a knee that tells me when it is going to rain, a right ear that doesn't hear too well from all the shooting, and a fungus that has invaded all my toe nails."

He did have some nasty looking toes. Each toe nail was up to a half inch thick. On summer evenings he often went out to the back porch steps and cut his toe nails, but he would leave the nail clippers in the house. His weapon of choice was a pocketknife, which he kept sharpened like a razor just for the purpose. He would cut his nails the way you might whittle wood.

"This is what happens when you don't take your wet boots off for a month or two and sleep underground," was the explanation he gave me for the funny toes.

He forgot to mention another thing he learned in the war—ping-pong. He was the best ping-pong player I had ever seen, and the only one I knew who held the paddle upside down.

"I did two things in the hospital in England. Smoke and play ping-pong as my knee healed. They didn't have surgery like they have today, so they just immobilized it and hoped it would heal. By spring, they could have braced up the knee and sent me back to the fighting but by that time my outfit was already near Berlin and the war was almost over. Plus it seemed that the doctor didn't have the heart to send any of us back. No one complained. We played ping-pong and I smoked so many free cigarettes that I nearly coughed out a lung every morning."

My dad had set up a ping-pong table in the basement and in the winter we played all the time. My sisters and I got pretty good but none of us could match the spins and "english" my dad put on the ball. The ball seemed to do magical things on his command.

"I learned the 'english' from the English," he would always say.

"When did you stop smoking?" I asked as I had never seen my dad with a cigarette in his hand.

"I came back to the U.S and I was put in a hospital in California. On the day of my discharge to go home, I'm crossing the Golden Gate Bridge in an open jeep. We're all sitting on top of the seats, the cool ocean air is filling my lungs, and I take my half-smoked pack of cigarettes and toss it off the bridge. Haven't had another since."

These were the kinds of stories my dad told. They were interesting but never the types of things I wanted to hear. I wanted to hear about the blood and guts, I wanted to know how many Krauts he had shot and some real battle scenes, but instead I got the funny stories.

"How many people did you shoot?" I asked excitedly like a hungry wolf with the smell of blood. My dad looked out the window for a second or two and then looked straight into my eyes and paused, causing me to look away. Men and boys don't hold onto a stare unless they want to fight. After a brief moment I glanced cautiously back into his eyes and he gave me a little smile, which broke the tension.

"Oh," he finally said and then paused, "Oh, I don't know."

I knew that this was the end of the conversation.

Each year my dad had his annual bowling party and it often was at our house. The bowling parties had lots of whiskey and brandy, raunchy jokes, and roaring laughter. I loved it. At one of the parties, well into the night a couple of the guys started swapping war stories. I listened with keen interest from the darkened corner of the room. The stories were funny at first, like my dad's stories, but soon the laughter died away, the mood became serious, and the words somber and hushed. These were the types of stories I liked to hear, but I had to strain to make out all the words. I wondered if my dad would volunteer a battle story, but he didn't, though he was an attentive and concerned listener. But one old G.I. told some stories that had us all captivated.

Mr. Jackson always walked differently. Not a limp exactly, more like the bottom of his feet hurt. I never saw him complain about his legs, nor had I ever seen him stay away from any activities, so I presumed that this was simply his God-given way to walk. That night I learned that his legs were frozen during his time as a prisoner of war. Someone asked him how he had been captured and that opened up a flood of grisly and terrible stories that he told in a matter-of-fact way. I sat like a mouse in the corner, hiding in the shadows. My dad glanced over to me and for a second I thought he was going to send me away, but instead he gave me a little, sad smile and then turned his attention back to Mr. Jackson.

He was in a German work camp and they were either working or moving to another location everyday. On the coldest nights they would sleep three deep and rotate every hour, and Mr. Jackson told us that he looked forward to the time when he would get to sleep in the middle, and the only warm spot created by the body heat of the men above and below. While they were being transported by rail, they would use the rotation system even during the day just to keep from freezing. Almost everyday, however, U.S. or British planes would fire on the railroad cars and many of the guys on top of the pile would be shot. For each raid he was just lucky enough to be in the middle or bottom. His legs were frozen during his time in the work camp. He couldn't show any signs of pain because if you could not work you were shot. When they were liberated the hospital staff wanted to cut his legs off but he convinced them to leave them alone, which accounted for his strange way of walking.

I glanced over at my dad during the stories and he sat listening virtually without expression. I had to pee so bad that it hurt but I didn't dare move. When you looked at Mr. Jackson or any of the guys on the bowling team you would have never guessed that they were once warriors who had endured great hardships on the battlefield. The only thing that made Mr. Jackson stand out was that he was always slightly better dressed than most of the guys. When my dad would be wearing a dress shirt he would have on a sport coat. When my dad wore his sport coat Mr. Jackson would be wearing a suit and tie. He also was a rotten bowler but neither he nor the rest of the team seemed to mind. He didn't bend his knees and he dropped the ball awkwardly causing it to bounce several times as it traveled toward the pins. I guessed that he most have been a much better bowler before the war.

I was hoping that my father would volunteer a story but it didn't happen that night. The next day after dinner I was sitting with my dad at the kitchen table. I asked him, "Did you see any action like Mr. Jackson?"

"He had it a lot worse than me."

"Tell me a battle story," I begged. He was quiet for a few seconds, staring out the window, but then to my delight he started with a real story.

"We were at a place in France right on the German border. A place called 'Metz.' We were on night patrol. It was dark. Jeez it always seemed dark." He paused, lost in his thoughts staring straight ahead. He finally looked down at me with sad eyes and said, "Nothing more boring than hearing your old man's war stories. Let's play catch."

Chapter 5

Playing War

The next best thing to hearing a soldier's tale about battle was playing war. Our favorite wintertime game was sledding war, which was more like an air force dog fight; two sleds engaged in combat, one wins and the other crashes. In the summertime, we became foot soldiers in brutal hand-to-hand combat decked out in our plastic helmets, "child-safe" knives, and authentic looking military guns. Some kids had the more modern, Vietnam-like rifles but I preferred the WWII era M1 like GI Joe and my dad used. "It shoots as fast as you can pull the trigger." Not all the kids, especially the older ones, went for this game because it required quite a bit of imagination and there was no real violence involved. But I had imagination to spare, and a few of us could play the game for hours, ducking behind trees, diving into foxholes, bursting into abandoned buildings, and sneaking up on the enemy at night.

The GI battles took place behind our house in the woods, a mix of towering maple trees and long forgotten fields, which were slowly being reclaimed by the forest. The land was owned by the mining company, but early residents of Alpha cleared the fields in their spare time with buck saws and a borrowed team of horses. They supplemented their meager incomes with a small garden, a milk cow, or some chickens. There was also a scattering of apple trees, blackberry and raspberry patches now left to grow wild in places that only we knew about. In the late summer or fall we might get pinned down by enemy fire in a blackberry patch and indulge in the spoils of war.

There were never any fatalities in our group but we were often wounded. Most of the injuries were scrapes and bruises from jumping out of trees, crawling through a thorny berry patch or diving into foxholes, which were in ready supply courtesy of the mining company. I had the worst injury one summer when I tried to dive under an old barb wire fence to avoid a German air attack. Only about half the fence posts were still standing and the barb wire had been breached by fallen trees and time. The fence wasn't much, at best a single, rusty strand still connected to a few cedar posts. We all ran for cover when someone yelled, "Air attack!" and imaginary bullets whizzed past our heads. Everyone survived the assault without injury except me. I dove head first under a single visible strand of the barb wire fence and hit a loosely connected strand hidden in the foot-high grass. The wire pushed back my helmet and a rusted barb bit into my forehead near my hair line and ripped a jagged wound to the top of my head as my momentum carried me forward. I heard the wound before I actually felt it; a crunching, ripping sound. One of the adjacent fence posts that was lying on the ground sprung to life as the wire became taut. I immediately knew what I had run into. I rolled over on my back and the wire danced back to life, the old fence squeaking rhythmically like an old rocking chair. The single rusted barb that did the damage waved in front of my nose with a wad of my black hair.

I stood up and could already feel the warm blood moving slowly through my hair creating a tickling sensation. I touched my fingers to the wound and when I looked they were covered with blood. I showed my bloody hand to my friends, they grimaced and we started walking for home. By that time, two streams of blood had now made it to my shoulders, one down my forehead past my nose and over the corner of my mouth. My tongue instinctively took a taste of the warm salty stream. The other blood trail was running faster from around the top of my head and came down behind my ear. It took just a couple minutes to walk to my house. My mom saw us coming across the yard and she met us on the steps with a dish towel and a concerned look.

"What happened?" my mother asked as she dabbed my face and then my head with the dish towel, already damp from kitchen work, looking for the source of blood. "Did you chip a tooth?"

"I dove into a barb wire fence," I said as she inspected the wound. This was my third head wound this summer so my mother had lots of experience. The first came during a game of Jarts, the lawn dart game that has long since been banned because of incidents just like mine. Someone threw a wayward Jart and I caught it right in the cheek as I turned away at the last second. The dart, which had a dulled tip, made a round puncture wound that went all the way through my cheek save the thin membrane inside my mouth. I could still, nonetheless, taste blood in my mouth. It was a hard wound to clean and months later, after it had healed over, small pieces of sand migrated their way out.

The second head wound for the summer occurred during a game we created with an old inner tube from one of the large trucks from my dad's work. Although it was covered with patches it still held enough air for our purposes. We jumped on it like a small trampoline or rolled it back and forth, but the most exciting game was when we curled ourselves into the center of the rubber dough-nut and tried to roll down the hill. To go more than one revolution required a combination of flexibility, balance, strength, and courage and Karen was the best at it and she could roll the furthest down the hill. With practice, however, I got better and one day I made it all the way down to the alley, maybe five or six revolutions. Unfortunately, by the bottom of the hill I had lost my orientation because of the spinning and I fell out of the tube on my head, splitting open a gash when I impacted the gravel in the alley.

The barb wire cut, however, was the biggest bleeder of the summer and the dish towel was red with blood and my mother told me to hold it firmly on the wound as she went in the house to get more supplies. She came out with her medical kit and Karen holding more towels. Karen looked concerned, which made me worried. If our kids got any of these cuts today I suppose we would go to Urgent Care, but I don't recall that ever being discussed as an option for my various injuries. Like battlefield medics, mothers during this time seemed ready and able to treat a variety of injuries. Our frequent trips to the doctor today with every little ache or pain for us or our children make us forget that our bodies have remarkable recuperative power.

"Was this an old rusty fence?" my mom asked.

"Yup."

We held the towels in place for a few minutes but the blood seemed to turn off like a faucet, giving my mom a chance to inspect the damage.

"Karen, hand me that bottle," my mom requested. It was hydrogen peroxide, my mom's favorite weapon against infection. I had an infected ear one winter and she poured some right in. The popping and explosions in my head, according to my mom, meant that it was doing its job.

She put some peroxide on a towel and started dabbing the wound, but my thick mop of black hair and coagulated blood got in the way of proper application. "Close your eyes," she said as she started pouring it right over the top of my head. I could hear and feel the peroxide, "doing its job."

After half a bottle of application I peeked at Karen through one squinted eye. She gawked at me with a look that combined horror and amusement. "It's turning his hair white!" she yelped. I looked up at my mom who stopped pouring to look at the rest of my hair. She had been too busy pouring on the peroxide and watching it do its work that she missed the secondary effect of the liquid.

"Oh my," she said. Karen smiled and started to laugh. "Don't worry, we can just get the white hair cut right off," my mom said with a grin. "I'm so sorry," she said when she took a good look at me and then started to really laugh. I jumped up and ran to the mirror. I looked like a skunk. My black hair had three white streaks that I could see. My mother was right behind me. "As soon as we think the bleeding is done we will take you to the barber."

I had to take a week or so off from playing war and by the time I got back, sporting a much shorter hair style, my war-playing friends had a new battle plan. Dig in.

In the field right next to the steepest part of our sledding hill was an enormous boulder, which geologists refer to as a glacial erratic. Long ago this was a field used by someone for cultivation and rather than trying to move the huge rock they just piled more around it. Each spring farmers have to pick up the rocks that the winter frost has driven to the surface.

"Every time you find an enormous boulder like that," my dad once told me, "you'll find sand." He showed me the grooves scored into the boulder by the glaciers, which also dumped the sand conveniently for the people of Alpha who excavated it from the hill for their cement work and yard projects. The sand was much different than the rest of our local dirt, which was hard, rocky, and iron-ore red.

Although the sand had a reddish tint, it was clean and soft and easy to dig. By the time I got involved in the tunneling, two friends were already committed. They had a tunnel in the side of the hill that was deep enough to hide two of us. We took turns doing the digging while the other two removed the back dirt.

One of my friends was in the hole while Joey and I pushed the sand away from the opening. The late summer air was cool even though the sun was hot. If you stopped working, the sweat on your back dried quickly and gave your body a refreshing chill.

I had my back to the digging when I heard a dull thump and then a blood curdling but muffled cry. The tunnel had collapsed on our buddy. We jumped on the pile to save our brother but before we got there he stood up shaking his head and spitting out sand. The sand was dry and didn't cling but still he was covered. The worst part was all the dirt that had gotten into his pants, which were likely handed down from his brother and too loose for him. The only way to get out the sand was to strip down to his underwear.

After he got cleaned off and settled down we surveyed the damage. All that was left from our hard work was a half-filled in ditch and disappointment. I assumed that our tunnel digging days were probably over until one of us came up with an ingenious idea. There was a rotting tangle of old lumber that someone had dumped long ago, and we took one of the better boards and laid it across the half-filled ditch. Eventually we covered the entire ditch with boards and then finished it off by concealing them with dirt and chunks of sod. In short time we had resurrected our small underground tunnel and had a new plan of action.

For days afterward we dug ditches and covered them with boards we scavenged from around town. We got better about concealing the boards by fitting the sod back into place and soon we had a labyrinth of tunnels completely hidden from view. When the tunnel became too dark to see, we would put a pencil-width size hole in the roof, which would let in a beam of sunlight.

We had countless hours of fun. On some days we were prisoners of war escaping the German stalag by burrowing under the fence and guard towers, and on other days we would dive into the tunnels with our knives clenched between our teeth rooting out the Viet Cong who had created a city of underground tunnels and caverns. We found some longer boards that we used for the roof of a larger room that could easily fit all three of us. We would stay underground for so long that when we finally did come out we had to cover our eyes for a time until they got accustomed to the sunlight.

One morning my mother was stripping the sheets off my bed and she called me into my room. "Jimmy, where does all this sand come from?"

I looked at the exposed sheet, and it looked more like a beach towel after a long day at the lake. "We're playing in the sand near the bottom of the hill."

"Why does so much sand get in your bed? My goodness, you need to clean up better," she demanded.

Cleaning up better wouldn't help much, I knew. I got all the sand off my body but my scalp was covered with a thin layer of sand that was hard to get out. I took a bath just once per week in the summer and when I did the bottom of the tub had so much sand that it wouldn't go down the drain. I had to rinse the tub out a couple of times to wash away the evidence. My head would itch after a day of digging and when I scratched, my nails would get filled with sand. One morning while I sat eating my breakfast, peanut butter and bananas on toast, my mom walked past and gave my head a loving rub, which stopped her in her tracks. She turned around and parted my hair and peered in like she was looking for head lice.

"Jimmy, why is your head full of dirt?" she barked. "How do you get all this sand on your head?"

"We're doing some digging."

"What do you mean, 'digging?'"

"We're digging some tunnels on the side of the hill."

"Tunnels!" she screamed.

Underground tunnels have a bad reputation in a mining town and especially in our family. Not only had my grandpa on my father's side been buried alive, but my mother grew up hearing the story about the great Mansfield Mine disaster. We often visited the place of the biggest mine disaster in the county. I would stand next to the wide spot in the river that was once an underground mine and read the plaque every time I visited. "Twenty-seven men perished when the wall of the mine shaft collapsed and the river came rushing in." The men who made it out were working at over 40 stories below the earth. Most of the mine shafts were below the river and on September 28th, 1893 the weight of the water was too great and it caved in the upper galleries. All of the men were working far below and they knew something was bad because the rush of air blew out their candles and lanterns. Those who made it out alive, 21 in all, were at the lowest level and had to climb over 400 feet of ladders in the total darkness with water rushing in around them. My great-grandfather, my mother's grandfather, was scheduled to work that fateful shift but he was ill. He got a friend to work a double shift to cover for him and his friend was one of the 28 who made the mine his watery grave. The mine was never reopened, Mansfield became a ghost town soon thereafter and my mother and her side of the family were left with a healthy fear of underground digging.

"No, no," I said, "they're safe. There are just ditches with boards on top."

"Hmmm," is all she said.

This was the beginning of trouble for our tunnels. Soon all the parents knew about our handy work and it didn't take long for some parents and even our village custodian and constable to take a look. He always wore a blue Sears and Roebuck work cap slightly back on his head. When he took off his cap to scratch his head, which he did for effect more than to scratch an itch, you could see that he put it back on to the same place every time as a suntan and dirt line marked the spot on his forehead. He almost always had a pinch of Copenhagen snuff inside his lower lip, but he was such an experienced chewer that he rarely spit. You had to know where to look to see the chew and most people probably didn't even know it was there. I'm sure that our constable and custodian and all the visitors were surprised to see how much tunneling we had done and how our work was so cleverly concealed on the surface.

Concern for the tunneling seemed to be dying down until it was brought up at the next village board meeting. Our understanding was that some of the board members thought that the tunnels were quite safe and that this was good clean fun for us kids, but others thought that it was a safety issue as many people used the field for snowmobiling. I didn't see this as any more of a hazard as someone taking two pickup loads of sand out of the side of the hill or dumping a pile of scrap lumber full of rusty nails, but the safety argument carried the day. In a small group it takes one vocal person to sway the opinion of others especially if they have safety and fear on their side. Ironically, this was one of the safest activities we participated in and we were doing it in full view of the town folk. Far dangerous playing took place out of their view.

One of the most exhilarating games was jumping off the edge of the Judson Mine open pit, located just south of town. At one time a sturdy fence surrounded the open pit but falling trees and curious boys made it easy to breach the fence long before my time. I am unsure how deep the pit is, but if it is like others it could easily be 200 feet deep. It filled with water right after it was abandoned and its clear inky black surface made it seem like it was bottomless. We would drop large rocks in and watch them fall out of sight.

On one side of the pit was a sandy knoll that rose about 30 feet above the water's edge. The embankment was so steep that you could only go down it by sliding on the loose sand that would avalanche down towards the water-filled pit. If you took a running start off the edge of the pit you could fly for a considerable distance without ever getting more than a couple of feet above the sand. It was a lot like ski jumping in that you fly a great distance but never go too far off the ground. The landing was soft as you usually went up to your knees in sand, but it was a bit frightening launching off the side because all that you could see when you pushed off was an inky black abyss. We would, of course, have flying competitions with the most daring leapers coming close enough to the pit's edge to get a wet shoe. Tunneling, it seemed to me, was far less dangerous than this game.

And we really didn't have to dig tunnels if we wanted to do some underground exploring as old mining towns have more than their share of subterranean possibilities. We found one tunnel not too far from the Judson pit. It probably wasn't a mining tunnel but rather some type of utility or drainage tunnel long since abandoned. I didn't spend too much time in this tunnel because a day or so after I went down for a peak someone decided to light a camp fire. They got out safely but not before the volunteer fire department had to respond to a call about smoke coming out of the ground. Soon thereafter it was capped to keep out curious boys.

Certainly constructing our own tunnels was far safer than finding and exploring long abandoned tunnels, but the village board didn't see it our way and we had to destroy the work that had provided so many hours of fun. No more games about tunneling out of Stalag 13 or chasing Viet Cong into their underground labyrinth. I was distraught. My mother tried to explain that they were not trying to spoil anyone's fun, just wanted to make sure that no one got hurt. But she didn't understand that people get hurt in war, that is just part of the game.

"How come dad never talks much about the war?" I asked my mother seemingly out of the blue. She didn't see the connections between tunneling, sled riding or other games and war. It was back then, around 1968, that I started to really wonder about the war. On this and several occasions since, she told me that my dad didn't really tell her much about the war either. They married in September of 1945 soon after he got out. Although he walked with a limp when he got home, he didn't complain about it and never said much of anything about the experience. My mother asked about the war on several occasions, but he would simply say, "The war's over," and that would be the end of the discussion. My mother had no reason to push and it was a new and exciting time in their life, buying a farm and starting a family.

About two years after the war, however, my dad's captain, Don Keller, wrote him a long handwritten letter. Capt. Keller was the Battery D (Dog Company) Commander of the 119th AAA Mobile Gun Battalion, and he received a Bronze Star for his actions on August 1st, 1944 near Vezins, France. My dad let my mother read Capt. Keller's letter and she remembers it being warm and affectionate. But my dad put it aside without comment and they forgot about it. They had just purchased the farm and my dad was working all day and some nights for the dairy hauling milk and trying to get the farm going too. A few months passed and my father received another letter from Capt. Keller. The second letter said how he appreciated my dad, what a great soldier he was, and things like that. He wondered how my dad was doing, how his leg was healing and whether he had a good job. He invited him to come and stay with him in Los Angeles if he ever got out west and to let him know if my dad needed anything. My mother encouraged him to write Capt. Keller back. "Nah, the war's over," is all he would say.

Dog Battery was one of the few groups to have a published combat diary. At the end of the war they had some down time in Germany and the diary was published in July, 1945 in Regensburg, Germany, and it was distributed to all the men in the company. The book is, in large part, a matter-of-fact chronicle of their movement, the number of rounds shot out of the 90 mm gun, and funny events that happened during the countless hours between battles. Private Steve Rudish sprained his ankle badly in a crash of a German motorcycle he was driving while he and Hansen were "cavorting about the French countryside in search of a little diversion." As is common in combat diaries, death and brutality are downplayed. On September 26th, 1944 they turned their 90 mm cannons, designed primarily as an anti-aircraft gun, on German infantry that had dug 3000 foxholes. From point blank range "our fire was bursting 30 yards above the Kraut filled foxholes. The Jerries quickly began to evacuate their positions, carrying dead and wounded comrades with them, and we continued to paste them with more and more salvos of time fire." When the shelling was over they inspected the battlefield and found no evidence of life. Just one sentence after describing what must have been a grisly scene, the authors note, without any transition or even a paragraph break, that this was a nice place to set up camp because of the good showers and some of the guys from the group found a small café where they found watery beer but "delicious fried rabbit and good vin rouge."

In the larger picture, however, the irony of their battles across France was not lost on the authors of the diary. On October 3rd, while stalled along the infamous Maginot Line, they received word that the name of the 119th Battalion had been inscribed in the "Golden Book of Verdun," alongside the WWI units who had liberated this area. A comment on the experience drips with sarcasm: "Now we of another generation and another war have our names inscribed in the 'Golden Book.'"

My father is mentioned in two places in the diary, on the day he was injured, and in a section called "Thumbnail Sketches." The latter includes a nickname, maybe a description of the person, and usually a funny anecdote, though the humor of some of the inside jokes has long been lost. For a guy named Blood the entry is, "'Liberator'—Height Finder on Target—Blue eyes, What a form! IFF Clear—One Blonde passing by—'Remember Tonfanau.'" For Stephenson it says, "And also a boy who could tell you the name of any and all pin-up gals." But sometimes the sketch was short and humorless, as it is for Wohl. "His tragic and untimely death left a void in the hearts of all." The thumbnail sketch for my father is one of the longest. It says, "Skibo—'Bohdja'—The beloved Polack of the outfit was lost when he broke his right leg. His ulcers bothered him so that he could eat but 3 meals a day. A Michigan boy who was exceedingly popular with everyone." Elsewhere in the diary it states, "The complete, all enveloping, darkness of the French nights finally effected their inevitable results on Dog Battery on the night of the 11th of October. Sgt. Matthew Skibo "The Bohdja" was checking his guard posts at the Gun Park and accidently stepped into a foxhole. The result was that Skibo was lost to the hospital with a fractured ankle."

The nickname "Bohdja" was given because when barking orders to his mostly California outfit in his Upper Peninsula/Polish accent it would make "both of you" come out like "Bohdja." Bleeding ulcers kept my father in the infirmary while still in the U.S. before his deployment so he was not assigned to the Michigan group but instead became part of Dog Battery composed mostly of California boys. The broken ankle turned out to be a blown out knee and the foxhole in the description was actually an abandoned French well.

But before he was injured at Metz, which is in eastern France near the German border just south of Luxembourg, he and the men of Dog Company literally walked across France starting at Normandy and through towns such as Rennes, Le Manns, Orleans, and Reims. Today this would be a hiker's dream but it was a different hike in 1944. According to Stephen Ambrose, Metz was the most heavily fortified city in Europe, and it is where the Germans decided to take a stand. Dog Company was the first to fire on Metz and start what has been called the "unknown battle" because, in part, it was the first defeat and retreat of Patton's

3rd Army. After racing across France, the 3rd Army's advance was stalled at Metz for three months of bitter fighting.

Unfortunately, neither of the letters from Capt. Keller survived and my mother never asked my father about it again, respecting his wishes not to talk about it. And I eventually did the same. Yet, when the 50th anniversary of D-Day was approaching and there was all the talk of the "greatest generation," and many old veterans were returning to France, I asked my father, "Why don't you go back to France?"

"No," he said. "I have no interest in going back." I sat there silently giving him a chance to say something if he wanted to but he said nothing more. But it was during this year, and the constant barrage of television specials, commemorative magazines, and Tom Brokaw's book, *The Greatest Generation* that did get him to say one interesting thing. As the D-Day news specials on TV no doubt brought back memories, he said to both my mother and me on separate occasions something about the French farm animals. "You know one thing that bothered me? As a farm kid it was hard for me to see all these beautiful farm animals that were killed during the battles. They cleaned up the dead soldiers right away but the animals they just left to rot in their stench. I know that's kind of strange, but it bothered me."

By the winter of 1968, our destroyed tunnels were hidden by three feet of snow and mostly forgotten. But I didn't stop thinking about the conversation with my mom and the fact that my dad didn't want to talk about the war. If I was in the war, I thought at the time, I would talk about it nonstop. What was it about the war that made him want to forget? And it was impossible for me to stop thinking about it. War was all around us. Every night Walter Cronkite told us how many Americans had been killed, and now to that he added the coverage of the anti-war protests.

These were tense times. At school we practiced our nuclear attack drill, marching to the basement in single file. The older kids seemed to enjoy these drills and the break from school work, but not our class. You could see that everyone was afraid just thinking about a mushroom cloud exploding near our town. And then the teachers would ask if we had a supply of food and water in our basement or fallout shelter. I had seen it a hundred times on the basement shelves next to my dad's workbench. Glass jugs of water, a few cans of food, and crackers in an old ammo box. I picked up one of the jugs and rubbed off the dust. I imagined what it would be like with the five of us huddled together in the basement sipping on the water and listening to the radio wondering when it would be safe to come out. Other families had much better fallout shelters; special rooms off their basement with shelves full of food, radios, batteries, and lanterns. Our dust covered stack of supplies next to the furnace made it seem like we weren't prepared for the bomb.

"Do we have enough food down in the basement for the nuclear attack," I asked my dad.

"Oh, possibly."

"But it's just a few boxes of crackers."

"But don't forget that we have the canned tomatoes, pickles, and jam down there too," he said while smacking his lips. I grimaced thinking about eating pickles, raspberry jam, and stewed tomatoes on crackers three times a day.

"And our basement doesn't seem too safe. Won't the radiation just come right down the steps and through the windows?" I asked. He didn't seem to share my concerns.

"I'm not worried about it. Don't you worry about it either."

But I was worried. Maybe I would be lucky enough, I often thought, to be playing at a friend's house with a well equipped shelter when the nuclear attack started.

Christmas break was a time for the round of parties. I drank eggnog and red pop, and ate pierogi and chocolate covered cherries until my stomach ached. My parents and the rest of the adults gathered by the "bar," usually an impromptu collection of bottles in the kitchen, which gave us kids freedom not usually seen in our own houses. If we were lucky someone might slip us a glass of beer, which we passed around until it was finished. The first sip was almost too bitter to take and we all, except for a couple of older kids, screwed up our faces when it hit our lips. This night's party was at the Frizzo's, who lived just up the alley from us. If you were standing on our back porch you could, if it was a quiet day, hear someone yelling at you from the Frizzo's back yard, but we still drove because my mother and sisters wore dresses and high-heeled shoes. I was especially excited about this party as the Frizzo's son, David, was just home from Vietnam.

David was a small town hero, of sorts, especially to the kids like me. He was athletic, strong, handsome, and smart. He was a sports star in highschool and all of us kids looked up to him. David, like his older brother, enlisted in the Army right out of highschool. I felt safe and proud knowing men like that were fighting the communists.

The night was bitterly cold and I was glad that we drove the 200 yards to their house. Walking from just the car to their front door was painful as I wasn't wearing my long underwear and my dress pants were no match for the arctic air. My mom and sisters squealed and trotted up the sidewalk in their high heels trying to beat the cold but risking a sprained ankle. I resisted the urge to run ahead of them despite my excitement at seeing David after a couple of years. I wanted to hear all about the war, which seemed awfully confusing. Body counts, cities burning and protests on one side, and John Wayne and the Green Berets on the other. Maybe David would tell me the truth about Vietnam and I knew he must have some tales.

He was wounded in the war almost a year earlier and we had daily reports of his recovery via the Post Office. The reports were unclear about how he was hurt. We guessed it was one of the wild bamboo booby traps that we had heard rumors about. We even built a few booby traps of our own in the woods. Our best one was a pitfall that had thin sticks and grass over a hole made a long time ago by the mining company. At the bottom of the hole were bleached out cow bones, which we pretended were human, adding to the fun. We took turns as the victim, which in this case was always an unsuspecting Viet Cong who was about to get a taste of their own medicine. We walked casually down the trail into the trap where we crashed into the hole onto imaginary sharpened bamboo poles that ran straight through our bodies and led to a slow agonizing, scream-filled death. Richie was the best at playing the Viet Cong as he could walk right into the trap like he was strolling in a park, while I could never relax enough to look normal. I looked more like I was about to fall into a pitfall trap, get stuck with bamboo spears and die a painful death.

We were met on the porch by Mr. Frizzo, who invited us in and started taking our coats. We were all huddled together on the front mat trying to warm up and wipe our feet, when Mr. Frizzo pushed his head into our group and whispered, "Don't ask him about the war."

My dad nodded. I was confused and crushed. "Why?" I asked. My mother put a finger to my lips and shook her head implying for me to keep quiet.

I could see David across the smoke-filled room surrounded by a group of mostly old ladies who took turns giving him a hug. The ladies were doing most of the talking while he nodded and gave them a forced smile between drags on his cigarette. I didn't remember him smoking before. He looked a lot different than the picture that hung on the wall, where both he and his older brother were clean cut and proud, decked out in full military uniforms. Today he had a shaggy mop of red hair, a big mustache that covered both lips when his mouth was shut, and long side burns. He stood there uncomfortably, talking about everything else except the thing that was on my mind and probably everyone else's too. How could a person spend two years away from home on the other side of the world, have so many adventures and then stand here among the people of Alpha and not even mention it? This was incomprehensible to me then, and even today when I have some knowledge about what the Vietnam soldiers went through I still find it hard to understand. The experience clearly changed him forever, and that evening, filled with small talk about the weather and his bushy mop of red hair, was the beginning of my transformation as well.

I suppose David didn't talk about it because it was such a difficult time, or it was no one's business but his own, or just maybe he didn't want to burden everyone else with his problems. He likely didn't realize at the time that when a young man from a small town gets killed or injured in the war it effects everyone in the town. His choice, like my father's, was to endure the burden in silence. Yet their silence spoke loudly to me. On one level it was quite noble not to burden anyone else with his story. Yet I wonder if David would have dealt with it differently if he had known that the young boy watching him from the corner of his house many years ago would still be thinking of that day almost 40 years later.

I'm struck today by a similar phenomena during the war in Iraq. I had a tearful student come into my office saying that she would have to miss a few days of classes to attend a funeral in her small hometown for one of her highschool classmates who was killed in Iraq. I told her that was certainly OK and then asked her a little about the soldier and how she knew him. As it turned out, she didn't know him well, yet her grief was real. Like the ripples in a still pond from a dropped pebble, the death of any soldier, especially one in a small town, is much more than one rock sinking silently to the bottom as the rings of acquaintances quickly touch hundreds of people.

It wasn't long after the Christmas party at the Frizzo's house that tragedy would again strike our town. I don't recall how I first heard the news but it was likely through my mother who collected important information along with the mail Within an hour, I suspect, everyone heard that a guy we called "Chummy" lost both his legs in Vietnam as a result of a helicopter crash. We didn't know Chummy or his family very well but he and his father, brother and sister lived near the bottom of our sledding hill. When there were no leaves on the trees you could see the top of their house from our kitchen window.

When I heard the news I immediately thought of the last time I saw Chummy. I think it was a pickup baseball game of some type behind the school. He wasn't a very good baseball player but he was the kind of guy who didn't seem to care. I remember him playing left field and charging in to catch a short fly ball just over the shortstop's head. His penny loafers came flying off as he came charging in. He tripped and fell in his stocking feet, rolled over and still managed with a last minute lurch to get a glove on the ball, which then bounced off his shoulder and dribbled back into the infield. It was funny to watch but no one laughed harder than Chummy.

The news lowered a dark veil over our town. Unless there was some real news about Chummy's recovery, and there rarely was, no one talked much about the accident but everyone acted differently. Fewer smiles and less laughing at the post office, and our dinner conversation was not quite so spirited. Lack of real news, however, didn't keep any of us from passing around rumors and speculating about his accident and injury. Where were his legs cut off? Would they give him some fake legs? What did it feel like? How could he drive a car?

Several months later we heard that Chummy came home. There was no parade, no hero's welcome, we just heard that he was home. His house, at the base of a hill, had such steep steps that I imagine that he had to be carried into the house by his father or brother. Not long after his return, a robin-egg blue CJ5 jeep, specially outfitted by the government with hand controls, appeared in front of his house. This was the first brand new jeep I had ever seen and I was quite envious of this beautiful machine. The first time I actually saw Chummy after his arrival back into town was when he was driving his new jeep around town. He must have put a special muffler on the jeep because it had a sound of an angry dog, which I could hear roar to life when it started in front of his house. On many nights, at maybe 2:00 or 3:00 in the morning, I would hear the familiar sound as his jeep would have to growl a little while climbing our hill. Chummy would roll slowly past our house doing solitary laps around our small town. Sometimes I would get up on my knees and look out the window. He drove slow, probably in second gear, with the window down despite the cold, the glow of his cigarette illuminating his face. I would duck down low when he passed my window, though I'm sure he couldn't see me. Ten minutes later he would often come back again, having completed a slow, sad loop around the perimeter of our town.

The beautiful, shiny CJ5 jeep didn't last long as he rolled it when trying to climb one of the stock piles, which were the old tailings piles that surrounded each of our mines. A common party place, referred to as "the ponds" because it was next to Alpha's new sewage treatment facility, was located on top of one of the stock piles. There was a trail on the side of the pile, used by dirt bike riders testing their skill. Deep into the night during one of the parties, Chummy tried to climb the hill with his jeep and it spun out near the top, slid sideways and then rolled several times back down to the base. The jeep, though badly crumpled, was up-righted by the party goers and it still could be driven. Undaunted by his failure to scale the hill, Chummy tried the hill two more times, despite protests from his friends, and each time it rolled and flipped back down, with the roll bar the only thing keeping Chummy from being crushed. Miraculously, the jeep could still be driven after the three failed climbs and he would have tried again had his friends not pulled him from the jeep. The next day, after we heard the story, we rode our bikes past the jeep parked in front of his house. The body looked like a piece of tin foil that you crumble up and then unravel as there was not a dent-free patch to be found on the jeep. The once beautiful machine could still move under its own power but it shuttered and protested when it started and moaned when cornering, like a boxer the morning after a fight. At the time, I was, unfortunately, most upset by the jeep. I was jealous of Chummy for getting such a wonderful machine and unmoved by the sacrifice he had to made to get it. I was also upset that he would be so reckless with it. I didn't know it at the time, but such behavior is common among those coming back from war. He seemed to have a death wish, which continued into the winter months when he bought a snowmobile.

Both of Chummy's legs were cut off above the knee, making any activities that required lower leg support and balance, like snowmobile or horse riding, more difficult. Even a gentle horse and riding a snowmobile on a smooth trail without legs would be treacherous, but it was made quite dangerous by Chummy as he bought the fastest machine available. This snowmobile was altered for speed and was used in local races. Chummy got a good deal on the snowmobile as the previous owner was thrown from the machine in a race and paralyzed from the neck down. I met Chummy one afternoon on the mining company's old railroad grade, now used as a snowmobile trail. This was the first time I had seen the machine close up. The modified engine was louder than a rock concert and I had to yell just to be heard. "How fast does she go?" I asked. He answered by revving the engines a couple of deafening times and then blasting off down the trail. His strong arms were the only thing that kept him from flying off the machine as it hit the bumps. His butt was off the seat more than on as he disappeared over the hill, the roar of the engine still heard as he went into Alpha, maybe a mile away.

I will never know the true horror of Vietnam for those who served, but I did get another glimpse of it years later when I was in high school and working during the summer for the DNR. I worked with Joe, who was married to my dad's first cousin. He was one of the few who chewed long-leaf tobacco as Copenhagen or Skoal were more common. I always drove the truck and he would sit in the passenger seat and tell me stories, rolling down the window occasionally to spit. He was a colorful story teller and he would delight me with tales of my father's family and add more spice to the stories of my grandfather's earlier years. "Your grandpa," he'd say with a chuckle, "was one crazy son-of-a-bitch when he was younger. Did you know that he shot at a couple of kids who he kicked out of his party?" Of course I knew the story, but Joe had a far more entertaining way to tell it. He and his family lived just a couple miles from my grandfather's farm, and were also one of the original Polish immigrant families in the area. Joe also taught me to drink coffee and enjoy a U.P. specialty, fresh homemade pie made with local blueberries, blackberries, and raspberries.

Joe had opinions about every subject and would judge a person immediately. If he liked them he was their friend for life, but if he didn't like or respect someone he was quick to share his thoughts, usually under his breath so you had to be close to hear. He had a nickname for everyone, and some of the names were unflattering and never said in the presence of the person.

On one afternoon we were sitting in our favorite pie shop and heard a crash outside. One of the regulars, an older man, was making a left turn off the highway and turned into a delivery truck who was attempting to pass him. The impact sent the man's car off the rode and he hit a tree just 20 feet from where we were sitting. Joe liked this old retired guy so he and I rushed out to the accident. His door was caved in from the impact and Joe couldn't open it so he turned to me, and with two feet against the car I was able to bend open the door enough for Joe to reach in and turn on the guy's left blinker. From that day on his nickname for me was "muscles." The old man behind the wheel was shook up but well enough to come out and have a cup of coffee. When the police arrived and noted that the guy's blinker was still on he dutifully gave the delivery van driver a ticket.

On some days we would spend two or three hours driving to and from our work site, so there were lots of opportunities for stories about every subject. One day I told him about David after he came back from the war, and he then offered a story about his son, who served in Vietnam. He told me that when his son got home from the war he wasn't hurt but he acted strange for a while. It was July and haying season when he came home. Joe, like a lot of people in the area, were full-time farmers while holding down a full-time job. The rain had put them behind on haying so Joe had to get into the fields the day after his son got home.

"I told him that he could stay in the house and relax but he wanted to help out. I was running a tractor with the bailer and the boy was put on a tractor with the mower. A little deer fawn jumped up just as the sickle blade on his mower passed and all four of its legs were cut off just below the knee. I looked over and I could see him on the ground bent over. I thought something was wrong so I jumped off my tractor and went over to see what the problem was. About half way there I yelled to him but he didn't answer or move, so I figured he must be hurt. I started running over there. When I got there he was holding this little fawn in his arms. He was bawling his eyes out and holding the little fawn like a sick baby. I didn't know what to do so I just sat in the grass a little ways away. He held the fawn until it died. He then stood up and without a word walked off into the woods still cradling the fawn like a baby. I guessed he was going to bury it some place in the woods so I stood there for a while and waited. After a bit, I jumped on his tractor and finished up his mowing as he only had a little left to do. By then it was almost dark so I drove the tractor back to the barn. I went to the edge of the woods and yelled for him but got no answer. He didn't come home that night at all. His mother was worried sick but I think we were right to leave him alone, not that there was much we could do anyway. Just before dinner the next day he walked in the door like nothing happened. His mother was frying up some fresh morels that I had picked and he sat down and ate the whole pan. Must have been two maybe three pounds of mushrooms."

"He never said anything about it?" I asked.

"Nope."

"What did he eat in the woods."

"Probably nothing."

"Why do you suppose he ran in the woods like that?" I asked with a puzzled look on my face.

"I really don't know for sure."

What are the horrors of war? I suppose in war people do things that they are not proud of, but most old vets tell you that the hardest thing is losing one of your friends. This is easy for me to understand today, but it was a lesson that was lost on me as a young boy.

Chapter 6

Work Day

Jeszcze Polska nie zginela, was the toast my grandfather made when we came to dinner. That is, "Poland is not yet lost." Then we would all raise our glasses and say "*Nazdrovie*," which meant "to our health." According to my father, my grandfather had always said this toast. Although I didn't know it at the time, *Jeszcze Polska nie zginela* is the first line of the Polish National Anthem. On one level, this is a quite odd toast and perhaps an even more peculiar opening line to their national anthem as Poland seems to have been lost many times. When my grandfather left Poland in 1907, his home region was controlled by Austria and there are few places on earth that have had more invasions and occupying forces. The first time I would have heard my grandfather give this toast, Poland was under the control of the Soviet Union, and for my grandfather's entire life the public singing of the song was banned. But after looking up the entire song it made complete sense as both an anthem and as a patriotic toast by my grandfather. In part, the anthem goes:

> Poland is not yet lost
> while we live
> What foreign force has taken from us
> we shall take back with the sword....
>
> March, march Dabrowksi
> From Italy to Poland
> Under your command
> We will reunite with the nation.

Father, in tears, says to his Basia: "Just listen,
It seems that our people are beating the drums."

Poland, for my grandfather, wasn't on the map but rather in the heart of all the Poles, and their country is not lost if there is just one Polish person left standing.

Chopin, the early 19th century Polish composer is, understandably, one of Poland's greatest treasures. His music is said to encapsulate the suffering but also the hope and power of the Polish soul. The hope and resolve seemed very evident in my grandfather as well. Years after my grandfather died, Lech Walesa climbed the fence at the Gdansk shipyard and gave rise to the Solidarity Movement and eventually Polish independence. My grandfather was right, *Jeszcze Polska nie zginela*. Although grandpa wouldn't have been surprised by this uprising, I just wish that he would have lived long enough to see it. What might have surprised him, however, is that they took back Poland without the sword. Lech Walesa, who won the Nobel Peace Prize, and his supporters advocated nonviolence as a means to affect change in the spirit of Gandhi and Martin Luther King, Jr.

My uncle Caskey, a nickname for Casimer, was ever present at Christmas Eve dinners but always a mysterious figure. He was likely named after Casimer Pulaski, the Polish patriot and Revolutionary War hero. Prior to serving in the Revolutionary War, Pulaski was one of the eight original associates of the confederation of Barr, which tried to expel the Russians from the Polish homeland. After the confederation of Barr failed in its attempt at Polish independence, the Pulaski family estate was confiscated and he was made an outlaw with a price on his head. Their failed attempt led to the partition of Poland into regions controlled by Russia, Austria, and Germany, which is the Poland my grandparents were born into. Pulaski escaped to Paris in 1775, where Benjamin Franklin convinced him to join America's efforts for independence. Pulaski was commissioned by George Washington as a brigadier-general and then involved in a number of battles until he was mortally wounded as he led the American and French cavalries during the assault on Savannah. He died on October 11th, 1779, 165 years to the day before my dad was injured in Metz, France.

My Uncle Caskey always seemed uncomfortable at these gatherings, ate without saying anything, and then would leave as soon as he finished. My dad was the oldest son and Caskey was the next in line, which on a farm meant that they were given lots of work and responsibility at an early age. While their father did his shift at the mine, they were up before dawn to feed the animals, clearing land with cross-cut saws and axes, and plowing the fields with a horse when they each had to reach up to grab the plow handles. "And the ol' man would give us a spanking before he left in the morning just to get us motivated for work," my dad would say. Caskey and my dad seemed to have a deep bond, sealed in the countless hours of hard work and play. They would work hard to complete their assigned chores so that they would have time for their passion—baseball. Without gloves or shoes, never worn by kids in the summer, they would play in the field clipped short by the grazing cattle. Despite getting hit in the nose with a wayward bat, which forever gave his nose a slight bend, my dad played organized baseball into his 40s, quitting just about the time I was born. Although he was never a pitcher, he could throw a nasty curve ball that I had to struggle just to catch.

When my father was only 12 years old, he and Caskey had to stay behind to keep on eye on the Sunday dinner while the rest of the family went to church. One of their jobs was to make apple pies, but the rolled up ball of dough was just a little too much like a baseball and soon they were tossing it around the kitchen and hitting it with a rolling pin. By the time they were done the dough was filled with bits of dirt picked up from the floor, but they went ahead and made the pies anyway as time was now too short to start again. They made the pies and were quite tense through the entire dinner, anticipating a beating for their irresponsibility once dessert was served. But instead, "The ol' man," my dad liked to say with a twinkle in his eye, "went on and on about how good the pie was."

During the Great Depression, Caskey and my dad served together in the Civilian Conversation Corp (CCC), which was a work program instituted by Roosevelt. They lived in a military style camp about 100 miles away and only came home on holidays. Their paychecks, however, were sent back home to help support their parents and six brothers and sisters. Just days after the bombing of Pearl Harbor, they enlisted together in the military, but were split up with my father going to Europe and Caskey going to the Pacific. When they returned from the war, Caskey was my father's best man at my parent's wedding. He never married but instead stayed on my grandparents' farm and helped them run it.

I loved to hang out at the farm with Uncle Caskey. I would help him milk the cows and clean up the manure, adding to the immense pile outside the barn. One cow wouldn't give milk to the machine so my uncle milked her by hand. The wild barn cats would gather and sit on their haunches and wait for a spray from the cow udder. He was an accurate shot and each cat got their face covered with milk. They would spend the next 15 minutes licking themselves and each other off.

"Squat down here by me and open your mouth," he said to Karen and me during the afternoon milking. We did as told and got a splatter of milk in our mouths and all over our faces. The milk was warm, almost hot, and tasted rich and sweet. He threw back his head and let out a roar. He didn't laugh as often as my dad but when he did he sounded just like him. The finicky cow stamped her foot in disapproval and turned around to see what the commotion was about.

He spent everyday, sun up until sun down, in the barn. And even though he had bathed and had on clean clothes he still smelled like the barn on Christmas Eve. No one seemed to mind or even notice. I actually liked the smell, though the farm kids at school often got teased for smelling like the barn. My dad would tell me, "Those kids are up at 4:30 in the morning and they work for two hours before coming to school and the teasers fall out of bed at 7:30 looking tired. Who should be the ones getting teased?" I had the feeling that once you smelled like a barn going to school you tend to stand up for the farm kids.

A farmer's hands were easy to spot. When Uncle Caskey passed the pierogis, I could see that he tried hard to get his hands clean as they looked red and overly scrubbed, but they had creases and crevices that no amount of washing would clean. Though he always had gloves, especially in the winter, they were usually in his back pocket. Each of his fingers were almost as big as my wrist and his nails were split and beaten up from abuse. His nails were just another tool for the scraping and prying that went on everyday. He always seemed to have at least one blackened finger nail that had been caught in a gate, hit with a hammer, or pinched when trying to hook up a trailer to the tractor. When he'd get such an injury he would drill a hole in the nail to remove the pressure. Like my dad, he seemed unfazed by physical pain. My dad once told me that my uncle Caskey had a rotten tooth that was really bothering him. Instead of taking the time and the money going to a dentist he pulled out the infected tooth with pliers. This feat impressed even my dad and it made my eyes water just thinking about it.

We ate until we were really stuffed, yet the bowls of food seemed nearly as full as when we started, my grandmother's Christmas Eve miracle. My grandfather unbuttoned his pants, "to make room," and everyone's face was red from the rich food and the heat. The hours of cooking prior to the meal had put the house temperature over 80 degrees and the windows had so much steam on them that little drops had formed and started to run down in parallel streaks.

For a traditional Polish Christmas Eve dinner, there would be a layer of straw underneath the table cloth to symbolize the Lord's manger. After dessert the kids got to pull a piece of straw from under the tablecloth. A green piece of straw foretold marriage, a yellow one meant you would never marry, and a short one, an early grave. My parents remember this tradition but unfortunately it had been abandoned by the time I was around for the meals. Nonetheless, I still found my grandmother quite religious but not in a way that was familiar to me. She had lots of home rituals that I didn't learn about in my Baltimore Catechism. One of my favorites happened on New Year's Day when they would come through our front door throwing nuts in front of them to ward off the devil. "Seems like a waste of good nuts," my dad would whisper to me. They would come in tossing nuts, chasing away evil spirits and bringing us good luck for the year.

The kitchen was grandmother's domain, and no matter who entered she was in charge. She got up before sunrise and started a fire in her kitchen range, which was half gas and half wood. The small fire "got the chill out" on all but the warmest July or August days. She always wore a dress that hung midway between her ankles and knees, and the only time anyone ever saw her knees, according to my dad, was when she hopped into the sauerkraut barrel after she added a couple more grated heads of cabbage. She removed her shoes, hitched up her dress and stomped down the cabbage for about five minutes. Sauerkraut was served all winter long for every dinner simply by reaching in and scooping out enough to feed the family and any guests.

After dinner and dessert, I could see my Uncle Caskey putting on his jacket and hat for a walk out to the barn. He spent less time in the house then any person I knew. At these events he stayed just long enough and then escaped the first chance he got. I ran and put on my jacket too. It was surprisingly warm and the snow was even a little sticky. I never let sticky snow pass by without making and throwing snowballs. Uncle Caskey heard the door slam and he turned and waited for me to catch up. His dog saw me too and came bolting toward me. The dog had the meanest look when it ran and if I wasn't familiar with it I would have tried to get back in the house. But instead of attacking it came to a playful stop and immediately rolled on his back to get his stomach scratched. That only lasted for a second as he saw Caskey turn and start walking so he jumped up and bolted ahead. I raced to catch up too, gathering snow for a snowball as I ran.

The barn was on the opposite hill and we got there by passing over a small stream that they had long ago widened out into a pond. On the pond side of the road was an electric fence, which terrified me. On a dare I grabbed it once and was greeted with an awful feeling as electricity surged up my arm. I always assumed it would feel hot but instead it felt like vibrating bubbles traveling inside my hand and arm. This may have been the moment that I developed my somewhat irrational fear of electricity. Even today my pulse races a bit when I have to change a fuse. As a kid, I had a reoccurring electric fence dream. The dream I remember best involved walking home cross country and coming to an electric fence in the woods. It wasn't like the single-strung lines at my grandpa's farm. This one had three strands with the lowest one so close to the ground that it made it impossible for me to go under or over the fence. The fence made a buzzing and crackling sound and I could see corpses of deer and birds who had made the mistake of touching the wires. In my dream I followed the fence for days looking for a place to cross.

We walked past the evil fence, around the pond and into the barnyard and I could hear the cows as we passed the tractor with the front end loader used to move the cow shit. An old dump truck was near the barn door and its box was nearly filled with beer cans. Uncle Caskey pulled a beer out of his jacket pocket and drank half the can in a few enormous gulps followed by a thunderous belch. In the barn we were met by the familiar musty smell and a much warmer temperature from the heat of the animals. The wild barn cats peered at us from the rafters or darted into secret passages in the walls. We walked past the cows and my uncle gave the occasional cow a pat on the rump. I did the same. They were all chewing their cud, which made sort of a slurping sound. Their lower jaws went side to side like an old man with bad teeth. Most of the cows had a build up of green slime coming out of the sides of their mouths that sometimes trailed all the way down to the floor. There was just a narrow path between the two rows of cows and when a tail raised I knew to step back as it was soon followed by an explosion of steaming, splattering crap.

Although I didn't understand the full extent of it at the time, Uncle Caskey clearly had a drinking problem. Though he kept the farm running fine, he did it in a beer and brandy haze. My dad was several years older than Caskey, but looking at them you would have guessed that Caskey had at least ten year on my dad. My father recalled that he was never the same after he came back from the war. He got a bad case of malaria in the Pacific, and he had reoccurring bouts with it throughout his life. Ironically, Casimir Pulaski too contracted malaria during his military service. Caskey, however, also came back from the Pacific with a severe drinking problem. For years he kept my grandparents farm running smoothly but eventually the drinking caught up with him. I'd be in my grandparent's house just after dark and Caskey would come in from the barn and grab a bottle of whiskey. He sat on the steps that led to his bedroom and threw back one or two shots before he could sleep.

After my grandparents sold their farm, Caskey seemed quite lost. My father bought him a car because Caskey said that he couldn't get a job without one. A lack of a car, however, really wasn't the problem. Several times my father tried to get him into an alcohol rehabilitation unit at the local veteran's hospital but each time he was met with resistance. One time they even agreed on a time to be picked up. He was living in a one-room cabin and he was waiting by the side of the road when my father pulled up to take him to the hospital. When my dad's truck came to a stop, Caskey just stood there and didn't get in. As my dad got out of the truck Caskey bolted into the woods carrying a six pack of beer. My dad never saw him again. Caskey moved in with an uncle who owned a small farm. He had less than admirable intentions for Caskey, who got a bottle of booze or a twelve pack of beer each day for work done on the farm.

It was around this time that my Uncle Caskey's new caretaker came to our house, drunk, and started screaming at my dad about getting cut out of my grandfather's will. I could see my dad's jaw clench, his face redden, and a vein bulge on the side of his neck. I hid behind him but he waved at me to leave the room, so I ran to a window in my parent's bedroom where I could get a clear view of the action, just three or four feet away. My father took his thick index finger and jammed it so hard into my uncle's chest that I heard the thud. "Don't you ever come over here drunk," be said loudly but without hardly opening his mouth. My uncle responded by taking a step closer and challenging my dad, nose to nose. With a single, powerful thrust of my dad's arms, my uncle flipped backward out of the door, which my father slammed making a house-rattling bang. He landed on his butt just inches away from my window. He turned his head slowly and looked directly at me, and I quickly ducked away, shut the curtains and ran out of the room.

Caskey died soon thereafter but my dad didn't learn of his death until after he was buried. He had a paupers burial arranged by my uncle. Thankfully, the Veterans Administration provided the funds for a grave, but it is spitefully located in another town, across the Brule River in Wisconsin. My father was clearly sad that he couldn't save his brother and he certainly would have liked to have paid for a proper funeral. Even though they hadn't been close for over 20 years, the bonds that were created in work and play would last forever. A small military headstone now marks his grave, which is appropriate. He didn't die in the war, but he was a war casualty nonetheless. Until my dad died, he and my mom were the only visitors to Caskey's grave site, which they stopped at a few times each year. Just before Memorial Day they would bring flowers and pull the weeds that had grown around the stone. After such visits, my father would often re-tell some Caskey stories, spending most of the time on the fun memories, like the Sunday morning pie baking. He'd often end by telling the story of trying to get Caskey into alcohol rehabilitation. Here the stories would end. On more than one occasion my mother would lean over and say that he had done everything he could to save him. My father would nod his head but look sadly unconvinced.

Going to college forced me to meet people from other parts of the U.S. who grew up in different types of environments. It made me realize that our family and most everyone I knew from Alpha never discussed anything that had to do with emotions or feelings. So much in our family went unsaid. Everyone kept a relatively even disposition—never too happy and never too sad. This was probably an adaptive response to living through hard times, physical and emotional, but it was not a good thing for an impatient boy who wanted questions answered. "Don't be whining about every little thing" we were often instructed, preparing us to withstand life's difficulties.

There certainly is some truth to that as there is little time for complaining if you are working full time trying to survive. This attitude also makes for good football players as the best teams are filled with players who are willing to tolerate pain without complaint for the team—to play hurt. It also makes for good miners and loggers. Perseverance and physical suffering come with these jobs. And they are, of course, mandatory character traits for a soldier. A good soldier must be able to endure physical and emotional pain and to detach themselves from the grim realities around them.

After my father died I decided to learn more about his war-time experience and the things he didn't tell me. So I read a lot of books, scoured the Internet and talked to some veterans. My best source was my wife's great uncle, the late Lyman Diercks, who also served in Patton's 3rd Army and who was, in many ways, just like my father. His parents were immigrants, he grew up on a farm, and spent much of his first 75 years of life not talking about the war. He was a 2nd Lieutenant in the 43rd Cavalry Reconnaissance Squadron, and was awarded the Purple Heart and the Bronze Star. He didn't talk about the war for many years because he didn't feel that he had the words to describe some of the events and it was, even years later, still too difficult to bring back some of the memories. But several events in the last 10 years of his life got him talking about it. He became very involved in the Langlade County Historical Society. Members of the society decided to commemorate the 50th anniversary of D-Day by interviewing WWII veterans. In addition, local schools invited Lyman to speak to classes or students asked for the opportunity to interview him for school projects. He found it impossible to turn down the local kids trying to learn more about history. Finally, he was distraught to learn that some people questioned the actual existence of Nazi death camps. As an eyewitness to the camps, he felt compelled to speak out.

"My dad only told funny stories about the war," I told Lyman during a 4th of July celebration. "Why do you think my dad rarely talked about the war?"

"Some guys talk about the war all the time, some guys never talk about it," Lyman explained. "There is no right or wrong way. You've probably noticed that people don't talk too much around here. I've started talking about it lately, but there are still some things that I can't talk about."

I told Lyman about Capt. Keller's letters to my dad and his unwillingness to even write back. He nodded his head in understanding. "My dad would often say, 'The war's over.'" What did he mean by that?"

"Killing other men is not something you're proud of and not something you want to share with your kids. You have to become someone else to be a good soldier; like an animal or a machine. I did it and he did it because it was the right thing to do at the time. It doesn't mean that we're proud of it or we want to seem like we're bragging about it. He didn't talk about it because of the men he killed, but rather of the men, his friends, who died. He didn't talk about it because he didn't want to think about it and there is nothing he could do about it now. You know, 'the war's over.' And he knows that you wouldn't understand. Lots of his friends died over there; great men, great friends. When he looked at you he may have felt just a little bit guilty. He had a beautiful family and a long life. Those friends he left behind in France never played catch with their kids, taught them how to ride a bike, and didn't get a chance to see their grand kids. Soldiers who saw combat always have a little bit of guilt and sadness that is impossible to share."

Lyman could speak German and the part of Wisconsin he was from was dominated by German immigrants. I asked him if it bothered him fighting people who just might be relatives. As was his style, Lyman responded with a funny story.

"It was hard sometimes. There was another guy in my unit who was German and we'd often kid one another when we'd see a dead German soldier by saying, 'Gee, that's my cousin Otto.'"

"What did you think about the Vietnam war?" I wondered. He was a banker and I suspected that he would have been for the war. I was wrong.

"The guys who fight in wars, do the killing and see their friends get killed, are never happy about any other wars. A thought that kept us going during the war was that if we did our job and did it well, our kids, grand kids, and nephews would never have to witness such a thing. One thing that bothered me in the war was the way the captains and generals placed a greater importance on tanks, planes, and even ammunition than us men. So when I would hear that there is a ground offensive in Vietnam, I didn't think about it the way most people do, following the movement of troops on a map or keeping track of how many more people we killed. I think about the frightened young kids trying to take the hill."

My dad didn't talk about the war or anything that you find typically on Oprah, so as a kid I searched for opportunities to connect with him. During summer break I begged often to join him at work, and my relentless pestering would get me one or two chances. He was the road foreman for the county, which meant he supervised a crew of 30 who built and plowed roads, maintained parks, and built bridges. I could see that he was a good boss. He had a commanding voice, a stern look, a no nonsense work attitude and the willingness to pick up a shovel and help out when needed. His job was a boy's dream; ride around in his pickup to all the job sites, talk on a radio, watch big machinery at work, and chat with the guys. I can't ever remember being bored when I went to work with him.

One of my favorite things to do when I went to work with my dad was visit George, the carpenter, who could build or fix anything. He had a fascinating shop where he worked all alone. It was a working shop, cluttered, dusty, with numerous projects laid out everywhere in various stages of completion. His projects, however, were neat and made with a bit of an artist's flare. He made many road signs and I could always tell when we crossed the boundary into a neighboring county. Their road signs were on metal poles and were simple, usually rectangular, and plain. George's signs, however, were unique pieces of art made entirely of wood. My favorite sign style had jagged edges making it look like it was ripped out of the tree by some giant. Each of his park benches were different and carried his unique signature. My dad told me that George made some of the lake benches without nails or screws and they had lasted up to 20 years.

My dad would drop me off at George's shop while he did paperwork in his office. The sun would be beaming through a skylight illuminating a thick stream of dust all way to the floor. I loved the smell; a combination of wood, laquer, and glue. I marveled at his ability to take pieces of raw wood stacked in the loft and create impressive works.

As I walked in the door he immediately gave me a job that was "very important." I sanded or painted and he occasionally inspected my work and gave me a reassuring wink. His sawdust covered hat was always a bit crooked and his glasses would get so covered with dust that they did him no good so he would toss them aside, leaving him to search for them later.

"What do you want to be when you grow up?" he asked as we both continued to work.

"Ray Nitschke," I answered without delay. He was the only one who didn't laugh when I gave that reply.

"If I were you I would try basketball. Football may get you killed. But if you get big like your ol' man I'm sure that you will be a great football player if you want to. Your ol' man is quite a guy, you know. You'd do all right if you turned out just like him."

Just then my dad popped in. "Come on Jimmer, gotta go," he said as he came in out of the cold.

"You know what, *Mutchek*?" which was a Polish nickname for Matt.

"What's that?" my dad replied. He seemed to like George as much as I did.

"We got the next Ray Nitschke here."

"That's what I hear," my dad said smiling down at me.

George put his immense hands on my bony shoulders, squeezing slightly so that I could feel his calloused hands through my shirt. "He won't even need shoulder pads with these shoulders," George said.

"Maybe so but I think his mother might like him to wear them, just the same."

"Those women, always taking the fun out it, eh Jimmer?"

We drove for a half hour down a narrow road, rounded a corner and came on the work crew. A front end loader had a road culvert dangling in the air above a newly constructed ditch. They seemed busy to me but my dad thought otherwise. "Sure looks like they just got up," he said as he opened his door. He watched for less than a minute before jumping in the hole and helping to get the culvert properly placed. I stood and watched but I soon got cold and got back in the truck. It wasn't much warmer, but it was at least out of the wind. In less than an hour the culvert was in place and the front end loader was filling the hole back in.

The day was over when we got back to the garage. This was the favorite part of my day when the work was done and the guys would wash up and a few would hang around the pop machine. I think that my dad enjoyed this part of the day too. This was the time to unwind and the only period during the day when my dad seemed to relax. With his hat pushed back on his head, his legs extended, and his hands behind his head, he would prepare for the show. The guys would then begin to talk about their day and recount the funny happenings.

Of the four or five guys that often hung out, only Pops was my dad's age, though he looked a lot older. Everyone respected him for his skills as a driver of a grader, which, according to my dad, he could handle the way a surgeon handles a scalpel. He had a big gut and moved slow, but I had a feeling that he moved slow even as a skinny kid. Everyday Pops got a Mountain Dew out of the ancient soda machine, the kind that opened from the top and you had to slide the bottle along a rail before pulling it out. Pops ALWAYS got a Mountain Dew, which was an endless source for jokes.

"Pops, today why not get something different, maybe an orange drink?" Guido bellowed as he walked up. He was loud and one of the funny guys in the group. Everyone laughed though they heard a variation of this same routine everyday.

"Maybe I will do something different," Pops dead-panned. "Look here, I'm sliding the Mountain Dew out with my left hand," he said while winking at me. He always put a quarter in my hand and I always got a Mountain Dew too. Pops did everything slow including drinking his Mountain Dew. He brought the bottle up for a drink with a dramatic wide-sweeping arc and by the time he got the bottle half way his head was already arched back slightly and his lips were in the ready position. He always took three enormous gulps and then waited several minutes before repeating the process. By the time he was ready for his second round of gulping I was already done with my whole pop, which I drank in smaller but almost continuous drinks.

Once everyone had settled in, Guido or Toivo would tell a joke. I knew two jokes, which I had told many times, but these two guys somehow came up with new material daily. Guido and Toivo had contrasting but effective styles. Guido always went first. He was Italian and his skin got so dark from the sun in the summer time that Pops asked him if we had to worry about him starting a local race riot.

Guido told a joke with his whole body. He would act out the parts, prance around the small group and put so much effort into the joke that small beads of sweat would form just under his nose. He wasn't a big guy but he filled the room. I never thought his jokes were that funny but Guido would laugh so hard that I did too and so did everyone else. My dad would wait breathlessly for the punch line and then explode in laughter. Guido would then go around the circle and have a more personalized individual laugh with everyone, maybe repeating the punch line if necessary.

Toivo, a Finlander, had a much different style. He was as quiet as Guido was loud. Everyone moved closer when he told a joke. Toivo would sit and look at the floor most of the time, glancing up occasionally for emphasis. His jokes were often dirty and Pops would pretend to cover my ears when he got to the dirty part, though I could always hear just fine. Toivo would always raise his head for the punch line, which was met with laughter. With everyone laughing, Toivo would smile exposing his tobacco-stained teeth.

After the joke period, current events and sports were discussed. These days there was lots to talk about. The poster above the soda machine was a constant reminder that the Tigers had won the World Series. Al Kaline, Mickey Lolich, Bill Freehand, Storm'n Norman Cash, Willie Horton, Denny McClain and the rest of the team all smiled brightly in the photo. Looking at their faces I could almost hear the voice of Ernie Harwell calling the game from our kitchen clock radio. The Packers were always good and on their way to yet another Super Bowl. Although we lived in Michigan everyone in the U.P. cheered for the Packers. Each year my dad would get two tickets to the first game of the season from the local supplier of heavy equipment.

Lambeau Field was larger than life. I would convince my dad to go to the game at 10:00 a.m. when the gates opened, which meant we had to leave Alpha by at least 6:00 a.m. We were some of the first people in the stadium, a full two hours before kickoff, and the fall morning sun would just start to hit the field. The grass was so green and perfect that it seemed fake. We would walk around the nearly empty stadium, first on the bottom row and then at the top, where you could see and hear the fans already tailgating in the full parking lot. There were so many grills going that a haze of smoke hung over the lot.

The violence of Ray Nitschke's hits were best appreciated in person. His biggest hits were not on the players who carried the ball but on guys who tried to block him. I watched him the whole game. Even when the Packers were on offense I watched him on the sideline. Sometimes I even could make out his unmistakable whiskey voice, barking out orders on the field.

Years later I read a biography of Nitschke that painted a slightly different picture of him. Although by the time the book was written he had quit drinking and picking fights in bars, it seemed that in his early years he was a bit of a bully.

Today the conversation of the guys in the garage turned from sports to the war in Vietnam. Guido was saying how we should really kick some ass.

"Why don't they go in and really get those son-of-a-bitches." I nodded my head in agreement, as did most of the other men in the group. "We don't even seem to be trying. Why don't we really let them have it." Most of the guys except Pops and my dad were all too old for Vietnam and too young for WWII, but they seemed like they would have been great soldiers.

"What do you think, Matt?" Guido finally asked. All the men knew my dad was in WWII.

Yeah, I thought. Tell them dad. Tell them how you kicked the Nazi's ass. Tell them that if the WWII guys were fighting in Vietnam this war would be over.

My dad was no longer sitting with his legs extended and his hands behind his head. He had switched to sitting on the edge of the bench and he stared at the ground. All eyes were on him as he raised his head. He looked into the eyes of each of the men then said sternly, "Oh, I don't know." His eyes made one more sweep of the room and no one said anything else. One by one each man looked away from my dad's stare to the ground and began to shuffle their feet or fidget in their seat. Men and boys, like wolves, don't hold a stare unless they are prepared to fight. Finally, Guido broke the silence.

"Well, I better get going, the ol' lady gets crazy if I'm a little late. She thinks I might get a girlfriend or something." Others said, "Oh yah, me too," or "Yup, gotta go," as they left.

Chapter 7

Buying Scared

I was certain that we were both thinking of the incident as we drove home from my dad's work in silence. These were tense times at work and at home. International incidents beyond our control and thousands of miles away had become part of our small town world. It is one thing to face an enemy or a problem that was right in front of you and had some control over, but it is yet another to be dealing with issues for which we are all quite helpless. The news reported stories about men burning their draft cards or going to Canada to escape going to Vietnam, but that didn't seem like an option for any of the Alpha boys. Young men from big cities in California or New York my have exercised this options, but if our small town soldiers had such thoughts they kept it to themselves. Their fathers served in the military and, without question, they would too. Any anxiety they had about the war was overcome with the fear of being a coward, to embarrass their families, and especially to be less of a man than their fathers, who had, regardless of their role in WWII, become heros.

Interestingly enough, a common American responses to stress is to purchase something. I recall President George W. Bush encouraging all of us to do the "patriotic" thing and go shopping after the September 11th, 2001 attacks. But Americans don't need much prodding when in comes to the acquisition of material possessions. The desire to spend and possess is even stronger among those, like my parents, who lived through the Depression. After what seemed like a lifetime of handed-down clothes, patched shoes, and old cars and trucks held together with bale wire and ingenuity, there was a strong desire to purchase something new after years of post-WWII saving.

By the 1960s they were ready to spend and no purchase seemed more impressive than a brand new car. New automobiles, once an uncommon sight in Alpha, now were seen regularly. And they were beauties. The pre-WWII cars were black or gray, but the 1960s ushered in bold bright colors, like spring flowers erupting in the meadow after a hard, cold winter.

I have yet to meet anyone who enjoyed new cars more than my dad. He loved cars and he bought one almost every two years during my lifetime. Having no expensive hobbies, like golf or fishing, he indulged himself with Detroit's newest models. He was quite happy wearing the same pants for 10 years but he shopped for a new car constantly. Friday night shopping trips to Iron Mountain for groceries included a drive through the car lot, checking out the new models or just looking at the same cars that had been on the lot for weeks. I can imagine that the dealers moved the cars around occasionally just to keep it interesting for him. Every car salesman in two counties knew my dad by name. My mother tolerated such extravagance because it gave him great joy and he was frugal in all other things.

One afternoon just a couple of weeks before he died he was feeling a little better so he suggested we go for a ride. He insisted that we drive his Chrysler. We stopped for ice-cream and he was able to stomach just a couple of licks. The highlight of the trip was a drive through the new car lot. "Now THAT'S a nice looking car," he said with admiration. Some new innovations he didn't care for but most he accepted with enthusiasm. He adored his cars and he treated them with care. One of his last instructions to my mom before he died was to remember to change the oil in the car.

One of my favorite old home movies has me as an infant sitting on my dad's lap as we sit behind the wheel of a brand new 1960 Chevy Impala. It was a beautiful machine, baby blue with a white top. It had four doors to suit his growing family but also the V-8 engine and sporty design appealed to him. I look a little sleepy on his lap but he is smiling proudly—brand new car, brand new son. There is at least one shot of our car in virtually every reel of our home movies. In most cases he was the photographer and he would film us walking out of the house in our finest clothes and bonnets on our way to Easter Sunday Mass or some other event. In many cases we paraded to the car, which had been placed in the front of our house, where only guests parked, for just this occasion. We would parade past, proudly smiling and waving, but his camera always seemed drawn to the car, where it would linger a while panning slowing back and forth.

My dad didn't simply buy a car, he hunted them, stalking them all year long. In the fall most guys in the U.P. got "buck fever," as they readied themselves for white-tail deer season, but this time of year also brought new car models to the dealerships and my dad would get car fever. He seemed to prefer the Chrysler products (Chrysler, Dodge, and Plymouth) but over the years he owned Chevrolet and Ford products as well. After he narrowed it down to a couple of new models he would start the process of "dickering," going between dealerships working down the price. Even in off years, when he wasn't really going to buy a car, he would do some dickering just to keep himself sharp.

But in 1968, with cities burning and wounded boys returning from Vietnam, everyone including our family was in an especially heightened mood for buying. Even the Depression-era generation, who seemed more content saving their money, were inclined to spend a little more during this time. Maybe the world was ending so why not spend a little?

Bobby Kennedy was shot on June 5th, 1968 and several months later as soon as the new models came out we had a brand new Dodge Polara. This was the first time I went along for the buy. My dad paid for it in cash. It was the first fifty dollar bill I had ever seen and he had a pocket full of them. He let me hold one. It was the most money I had ever held in my hands at one time and it made my mouth go dry. I wanted to walk around the showroom with it but my dad snatched out of my hands, folded it around the other fifty dollar bills, put a rubber band around the wad and slid it in his pocket. It was so many bills that it made a bulge.

"How much money is that?" I asked in amazement.

"It's enough," is all my dad said.

"Is it $5,000?" I asked.

"Not that much," was all he said as he put a finger to his lips to keep me quiet as the salesman walked over. He liked to pull the wad of cash out of his pocket for effect once the deal got close. "I've got the cash right here," he would say. That was often followed by a walk toward the door and the salesman calling us back.

It was nicest car I had ever seen. The 30 mile drive home seemed to go by in an instant. When we pulled in the driveway my mom and sisters came running out of the house and Karen and Mary Fran jumped and danced around the car excitedly. My mom walked around it slowly, smiling, but with her hand over her mouth in disbelief. We got the camera out and took turns posing casually with one hand on the hood or pretending to open the door. It was a beautiful machine. When it sat in the sun, the paint job sparkled like glitter. It was a massive car but the power-steering let even my mom turn the wheel with just a single finger.

We went no where in particular that summer, but we put on a lot of miles just driving around. "Let's go for a ride," my dad would say, and we would all jump in. Sometimes we would end up at the drive in root beer stand for a treat but other times we just cruised around with the windows down.

Robert F. Kennedy was shot just a couple of months after Martin Luther King's funeral. Bobby Kennedy, according to people around town, was going to be our next President. We woke up to the news on the morning of June 5th, but he didn't die until a day later. We turned on the TV right at 5:00 to hear Cronkite report the grim news that went something like this:

"Senator Robert Kennedy, brother of the late John F. Kennedy, died this morning at a Los Angeles hospital as a result of the gun shot wounds he received early on June 5th in the kitchen of the Ambassador Hotel in Los Angeles. Sirhan Sirhan, a Palestinian, was apprehended at the scene and is believed to have shot the fatal bullets from a 22 caliber pistol. Robert Francis Kennedy, dead at the age of 43."

"Oh God, oh dear God," my mother kept repeating. My father sat there with his mad face on; jaw clenched, teeth grinding, eyes locked in an angry scowl. It was a mean look that even scared dogs. He was the only person I knew that wasn't afraid of mean farm dogs, which were there to greet you at almost every farm. Most people drove into a farmer's yard and waited for the owners to come out and calm the wild animals before opening their car doors. My dad would pop out of the car and walk straight towards the snarling, charging dogs, point his finger and bark, "Go lay down." And they did.

Another Kennedy shot. My wife and I share similar first memories and they both have to do with the death of John F. Kennedy. My wife was ill on the day JFK was shot and she was propped in front of the TV while her mother busied herself in the kitchen. News of the assassination broke into the regular programing and Becky went to her mother and told her the president had been shot. Her mother, thinking that the 3 almost 4 year old child was delirious from the fever sent her back into the living room. Soon thereafter, Becky's father called and confirmed that the President had been shot.

I have two first memories and I can't recall which one is earlier. One is the funeral of John F. Kennedy. I remember looking at my mom as she sat on the edge of our round naugahyde footstool, with her elbows on her knees and head resting in her hands. She was wearing short pants, in style at the time, that gathered tightly above the ankle and a white blouse that fit close around her waist. I thought my mother was beautiful and I loved to watch her. But on that day, tears streamed out of her red and swollen eyes and down her cheeks. In her hand was an overused tissue that she occasionally used to dab tears and to wipe her nose. I sat watching her while she watched our black and white TV from which came a slow, haunting drum beat. Although I sat in front of her, she stared at the TV like I was not there. I watched her while she watched TV, occasionally letting out a sad sigh. I stood up and walked to her side. I was about at her eye level. I was so close that I could hear her breath but she didn't know I was there, still transfixed on the TV. I pushed up against her side and she finally noticed me. She looked at me with her swollen eyes and forced a smile. She put her arm around me and pulled me in close. She finally told me that it was President Kennedy's funeral.

Our household felt a special closeness to the First Family. My dad and JFK were WWII veterans and were both born in 1917. My mom liked to say that she was about the same age as Jackie, but we were never quite sure how old that was. I was born in 1960 just like John Jr. and my sister Karen came into this world just a few months after the Kennedy's oldest daughter, Caroline.

The dream of everyone around our town was that Robert Kennedy would be President for 8 years followed by Teddy Kennedy. These dreams were shattered by one man with a small gun, a 22 caliber pistol, no less, one of the smallest guns you could buy. I shot tin cans with a 22 and most people used them for target practice or to shoot rats. I had no idea that it could so easily kill a man. It barely kicked when you shot it and it made a small pop compared to the roar of a 12-gauge shotgun or the report of the 30-30 deer rifle.

My second early memory is waving to my dad as he stood at the 2nd story window of the Crystal Falls Hospital, just a few rooms away from where my grandfather was left to die on the bed after he was crushed in the mining accident. In those days they didn't let kids into the hospital even to see their own parents. We all stood outside lined up neatly on the sidewalk staring at the window waiting for this orchestrated appearance like we were waiting to see the Pope in St. Peter's Square. The appearance was made to reassure us that he was OK, but when he came to the window I clearly could see that he was not. Behind the glare of the window he stood there smiling and waving but he was in a robe and pajamas. I had never seen my dad in pajamas and I don't think he owned a robe. He was up by 5:00 each morning and had his work clothes on before he left their bedroom even on weekends. He smiled at us and waved, and I waved back and cried. If they wanted to make me feel better he should have put on his work clothes. He was in the hospital for surgery on his stomach ulcers. Years later I learned that he almost died in the recovery room. My mother was called into his room after surgery and she was assured that all went well. She was permitted in so she could greet him when he woke up from anesthesia, but while she sat at his side she noticed that he started to turn blue and had stopped breathing. When she screamed down the hall, Dr. Addison came in and immediately and started CPR. He wasn't a large man so he was coming right off his feet each time he did a heart compression. My mother was ushered out of the room and then returned in 20 minutes or so to find my dad awake and alert.

My father's first memory also involved his father. My father was sent out to look for a horse that had not returned to the barn. My dad found the horse stuck in the deep snow unable to free himself. Farm animals tend to walk on the same trail and as the winter goes on they make a narrow, hard-packed path through the snow. The horse had slipped off the path into a deep snow drift so my dad ran back to the barn for my grandfather. They both dug, pushed, and pulled on the horse but the struggles just got the horse buried deeper as it slid further down the hill into even deeper snow. As the horse became more deeply buried my grandfather worked himself into an angry rage as the horse, too exhausted to go on, gave up any effort. My dad watched in horror as my grandfather grabbed his sharpened axe and with 4 or 5 hard swift blows chopped the horse's head cleanly off. I first heard this story when I was about college-age, long after my grandfather had passed away, and I recall sitting there quite speechless. To break the tension, my dad said that after he saw his old man do that he made sure that he never slipped off the trail. He followed this statement with his booming laugh and I laughed too, though a little nervously with the image of my enraged grandfather hacking off the head of a horse, the severed arteries gushing out blood and turning the snowdrift into a ghoulish red. His first memory trumped our memories of JFK's death and funeral, but certainly ours had more historic importance as this tragedy changed the world and especially everyone in the U.P. where mostly only Democrats resided.

Everyone in our county, it seemed, was a Democrat. "Even the Republicans are Democrats," my dad would say. My Grandpa Kania was chairman of Mansfield Township's Democratic Party and when they would throw an event at the Township Hall everyone would show up. Ever since Roosevelt, which people in my family pronounced like the beginning sound of "rooster," every elected official was a Democrat. Many people had a picture of Roosevelt on the wall right next to the pope, Pope Paul VI. Even though Roosevelt was a rich guy from a privileged east coast family he seemed to understand the plight of the poor people in the Depression. It was no sin to be rich, in fact everyone aspired to acquire great wealth, but it was a sin for an elected official to look the other way when there were children going to school hungry. My dad and his brothers and sisters went to school each day with a piece of bread covered with lard. Hunger pains were just part of every day. Roosevelt seemed to care and, most importantly, he seemed to have a plan to get the country out of the Great Depression. Our family's favorite Roosevelt program was the Civilian Conservation Corp. Both my dad and uncle Caskey worked in the CCC camps. They lived in military style camps, wore military uniforms and learned to live by the discipline of the military. Evidence of their work was everywhere; bridges, parks, roads, and public buildings. They worked year round and the government sent money home to their families. On our car trips we would often drive past something built by the CCCs, which would spark a memory in my dad.

"The CCCs built that," he would say.

"Did you like being in the CCCs?" I asked.

"Almost all the good public works around here were done by the CCCs. We were proud to be building something like this and it was nice to be sending money home to the folks and all my little brothers and sisters. There were no jobs so we were thrilled even though we would be away from home for up to 6 months at a time."

Every time I saw a picture of a CCC camp I thought it was a military camp. The workers were dressed in military uniforms and they stood in orderly rows in front of barracks.

"This program helped us get out of the Depression," my dad would say, "but they also prepared us farm boys for war."

I heard about the Depression every time my grandparents were around or when at least two people over the age of 35 were together for 5 or more minutes. My dad was about 12 years old when the Depression hit and it officially ended when he was about in his mid-twenties, but it did not recoil too far back into memory for the people of Alpha. Virtually anything that happened in the world or in anyone's life was immediately compared to the Depression for perspective.

"Someone lost their job? Nothing like the Depression."

"Isn't the food good today? Remember in the Depression this would have been enough food to feed an army."

"You think your bed is too small? In the Depression five of us kids slept in one bed."

"Your daughter has acne? Nobody had acne in the Depression. We didn't eat enough food to feed a pimple."

One way that a lot of local farmers tried to make ends meet during these grim times was to turn some of their surplus crop into something a little more profitable—moonshine. It was Prohibition. Before Roosevelt, right in the middle of the Depression when you really could use a drink, the government made it illegal to have a little brandy. I never met anyone who thought that this was a good idea and many turned to making their own alcohol. My dad liked to tell the story of the day he found the family still.

"I thought I knew every inch of our farm and the surrounding hills but one day I came across a trail in the woods that I had never seen before. Like any kid, you find a trail, you follow it. Down in the woods by the little creek I came across the ol' man's still. It wasn't much really. Just some barrels, a vat, copper tubing and a pile of wood."

"Finding the still was a big mistake. I went home and told the ol' man about what I had found and from that day on he put me to work at the still. I was the oldest boy so I had lots of chores already. So besides my regular chores I had to haul water, wood, and anything else that was needed, although they never let me carry the moonshine. But all that ended that winter when a federal agent busted the old man."

"One night a stranger came to the door. It was a cold night and he said he was a logger and made up some story about being lost. The old man was a little suspicious because it was odd to have a stranger doing any logging around here, but my mother always had a soft spot so she made him some food and put on some hot coffee. Then the guy says, 'You know what I could use, something a little stronger, something to warm me up.' My mother reached up on the top cabinet where the hooch was hidden and poured him a glass. He then pulls out a badge and says that my old man is under arrest. Boy, your grandpa sure let him have a piece of his mind about picking on the poor farmers trying to feed their families and so forth. You know how grandpa could be, he called him every Polish and English cuss word he could think of. They made the old man show him the still and the federal agents came out and hauled it away. That was the end of our moonshine. I was happy to see it go. No more extra chores. The judge went pretty easy on the ol' man. The only thing he had to do was a little road work when US2 came through the county past the farm."

Without the moonshine for income my grandparents had to find other ways to make ends meet. One way was to try to sell their extra farm products, like apples, eggs, and vegetables, in Chicago. My father, the eldest son, was given the task of driving an over-filled truck the 8 hours to the Polish neighborhoods in Chicago. He would unload and drive all the way back to the farm the same day, sleep for a few hours, help re-pack the truck and then do it again. This was kept up for several weeks in the late summer until the fall harvest surplus ran out.

My grandfathers' generation was able to find even more enterprising ways to make a buck or put food on the table regardless of the legality. My Grandpa Kania was skilled at snaring snowshoe rabbits, which were plentiful in the swamp just south of his property. He taught me how to snare rabbits, a practice he continued well after the Depression. He wasn't the only one who indulged because the local hardware store kept in stock a healthy supply of picture wire, which the locals simply referred to as "snare wire." I was in college with my first apartment before I realized the real function for snare wire was to hang pictures.

The secret to snaring, according to Grandpa, was to think like a rabbit, and he would spend hours crawling through the thickest swamps following the trails of the snowshoe rabbits. In the winter, when the rabbits turned white, they followed well worn paths through the swamp. The key was finding a spot where the rabbit went under a branch where the trap could be set. On one end of the picture wire you made an eye and when the other end was threaded through it made a noose. If you were good enough to set the snare at the right spot, the rabbit's head passed through the noose but when they tried to pull back the picture wire tightened, and the more they struggled the tighter it got. I set dozens of snares before I caught my first rabbit but I wasn't diligent enough in checking the snare so that if

I did happen to catch a rabbit, an owl or a coyote would get there first. All that remained would be the white hide, the only inedible part of the animal. My dad suggested that I not snare unless I could get into the swamp every morning.

So even into my teen years I would simply walk in the woods and pretend to be a trapper without the responsibility of actually dealing with a dead animal. I missed the thrill of the chase and trying to outwit the rabbits, but I enjoyed just walking in the woods. I admired trappers, who were independent, solitary, and hardy. They were the first to explore the Upper Great Lakes, searching for the elusive beaver whose pelt was fetching an enormous price in Europe, which the furriers made into hats popular at the time. Walking in the woods on a crisp winter morning it was easy to imagine that I was one of the hardy trappers, trudging through a frozen swamp, the only sound being my own breath and the gentle rhythm of my snow shoes against the fluffy snow. It was often so quiet that I could hear the hum of my own inner ear. When occasionally I broke this silence with a cough or the snap of a branch, the noise seemed to startle the woods as it held its breath waiting for the foreign noise to make its final echo off some distant hill.

On one of my walks when I was a teenager, I was getting cold so I crawled under the branches of a large spruce tree whose branches had bent to the ground under the weight of the snow. Once I had hollowed out some room under the tree by breaking away the dead branches there was enough room for me to stand, protected from the wind by the natural igloo. I started a small fire with the dead branches and it got warm enough inside for me to unzip my jacket. Such experiences made me feel connected to the trappers who had to battle the cold and find ingenious ways to solve the problems of everyday life.

Once the beaver had been trapped to near extinction, the woods themselves became the resource and the loggers took to the forests with the same hardy nature as the trappers. Logging was above ground mining that continues to this day. The white pine, maple, and hemlock were the land versions of copper and iron ore. Logging took place during winter so logs could be easily pulled out on ice-covered trails and then placed on the frozen river or lake where they awaited the spring thaw and their journey to the saw mill. Loggers had to be close to their work so they lived in camps, which were either family-run or owned and operated by logging companies. The company camps were owned by the lumber barons who clear-cut the forests leaving a waste land in their wake. The lumber baron camps were run like a military outpost. No drinking was permitted and there were strict rules of conduct and behavior that included, incredibly, no talking during meals. Working for the company owned lumber camp was very similar to working for the mining company.

The family run camps were hated and mistrusted by the big jobbers who didn't like the competition for labor or timber. The family camps were usually a group of brothers and cousins who worked for a month or so in the woods and did more selective cutting of the timber because they often owned and lived on the land that they were harvesting.

When I was 14 or 15 years old I got my first taste of logging as my dad had a plan to make a little extra money and also to "put some meat on my bones." He never said it but I suspected that he thought that my legs were too long and thin and my arms too spindly. The stated goal was to cut a railroad car full of peeled aspen, locally known as "popple," which my dad insisted on downing the "old fashion way." He cut down and trimmed off the limbs of the trees and I peeled them with a spud, which was a metal tool made from an old car leaf spring. For a month or so in the spring of each year the sap runs and aspen bark can be peeled off easily with a spud. After we peeled it, both of us then cut them into eight foot lengths with the devilish chain saw. After they dried some and were lighter, my dad pulled a drey, which was like a wagon on skids that he towed behind his little bull dozer. When we came to a fallen tree we muscled each of the eight foot lengths onto the drey where they were hauled out to the field and then muscled again onto a neat pile, making my thin legs and spindly arms protest.

I came to enjoy the logging but it did come with its hardships. My hands were bruised and swollen and the veil of mosquitos swarming around my head was a constant distraction. I wore the same pants for the several weeks of the peeling because they had to be thrown away once the season was complete. There was no way to get them clean once the sap from the trees mixed with dirt soaked into the pants. I stored my pants in the porch and they would get so stiff overnight as the sap dried that they could stand up in the corner.

But the most dangerous moment in the woods prompted me to cuss at my dad for the first and only time in my life. We were nearing the end of the day and my dad had "hung up" a big popple, which is one of the disadvantages of family-based select cutting—it is hard to drop a tree in the woods cleanly with all the other trees in the way. The big tree was cut off at its base but had refused to fall because it was lodged against another tree. The only solution was to cut down the tree that was causing the problem and my dad had already cut down two trees without any luck. The danger of logging came into play when trees fell in unpredictable ways, and now my dad was cutting down a third unnecessary tree. A beautiful blue spruce was the next fatality to my dad's mounting frustration. I was busy peeling but watching my dad with one eye as I could see that he was getting frustrated and reckless. He looked a little mad as his hat was on sideways as a result of getting wacked by a wayward branch, and his face was scrunched into a scowl as he attacked the trees with his roaring saw. I knew better than to intervene so I stayed at what I thought was a safe distance from the man that now seemed destined to make a small meadow in the middle of the dense forest.

With a loud crack the trees came crashing down. I turned my head in time to see the weight of the three trees come down against a relatively small but tall tree. For a couple of seconds the tree withstood the tremendous weight but gave way with an enormous force like the end of a bullwhip. The tree came whipping down towards me fast and straight at several times the speed of a normally falling tree. I was already on my knees peeling and I had just time to duck down behind the fallen tree, like a baseball player ducking away from a brush-back pitch. The quick move saved my head from being smashed like a watermelon hit with a baseball bat. I jumped up immediately bursting through the tree's branches, threw my spud down and launched into a torrid of fowl language aimed at my father's recklessness. With my arms flying and feet stomping I spun in two circles before finally looking down at my dad. He was sitting like a little kid when they kneel down and sit back on their legs. He had dropped his saw that was now sitting on its side and threatening to sputter out. My dad's enormous hands covered his face and pushed his hat off, which lay on the ground next to the saw. Seeing him like that drained the rage out of me. My legs felt weak so I sat down and watched him recover slowly. He sat motionless with his head in his hands for probably no more than a minute but it seemed much longer. When he finally uncovered his face he seemed much older. He took a deep breath and blew it out with puffed cheeks as he looked at me. I gave him a little smile and he nodded back just as the saw sputtered out. "Good job of ducking," he said finally. I nodded my head proudly hoping that he had forgotten the string of grandpa-like cuss words that had escaped from my mouth.

I don't recall that my dad ever cussed at me so I had broken new ground. He certainly had occasion over the years but none greater than the day he "taught" me to drive. We were on our property in the hay field not more than 200 yards from the tree falling incident. One of my dad's farmer friends had baled the hay into the dense blocks bound together with twine. The farmer was hauling the bales but could not get the last ten onto a load when it started to rain. My dad wanted to gather them up quickly in our pickup but he knew that I was not strong enough to hurl the 50 pound bales into the back of the truck. "Drive," he barked.

"I don't know how," I replied. The truck was a three-speed Chevy, manual transmission with the shift lever on the column.

"Haven't you been watching me drive?"

Indeed I had, so he drove to the first bale, jumped out and threw it on the truck and said, "Drive to the next bale." I got behind the wheel, scooted up in the seat so that I could push in the clutch and then dropped the column shifter into first gear. When I released the emergency break the truck started rolling forward so I eased the clutch out and I was indeed driving with my dad riding in the box. The field was bumpy causing the wheel to jump violently requiring all my strength to control as I pulled up to the next bale. My dad jumped off and effortlessly tossed the bale into the pick-up's box. He hopped back onto the truck and pointed to the next bale, which was slightly up hill. I released the clutch and the engine stalled. I started it up again and this time gave it some gas and the truck jerked into motion. I heard a low pitched cry that made me turn around in time to see him flying off the back of the truck. He landed on his right shoulder, tucked and rolled once and then popped up on his feet. He jumped back on the truck as I check the mirror in horror fearing that our driving experiment was over. Without a cuss or a word he nodded his head and waved me forward encouraging me to try again as he sat down on the bed of the truck and held onto the side panel.

Chapter 8

"Stand Back"

Not long after we heard about Chummy's injury in Vietnam my dad drove in with a new snowmobile, a bright blue Snojet. He came into the driveway with it on the back of his pickup and I ran outside without a jacket. I can recall just one other family in our town having a snowmobile and when they got it, a Skidoo, it caused a near riot among the kids. They got their snowmobile early in the winter and for several weeks a group of kids would gather at their house just to watch it start and take off. We soon devised a fun game of chasing and trying to catch the snowmobile. The driver, a highschool kid, would go in circles around a vacant lot and we would try to dive and grab onto the back bumper and get pulled along for a while. We were like farm dogs chasing cars. If we were lucky enough to grab on, the driver would try to fishtail the machine to shake off the attacker. No one could ever hang on too long, not so much from being whipped around by the driver but instead from getting sprayed in the face by snow and ice from the spinning track. I managed to stay on longer than most but soon I could no longer stand the snow in my face and down the front of my jacket and I would let go.

My dad backed his pickup to the snowbank in our alley and we all helped pull the blue snowmobile off the truck. It was surprisingly heavy. Without my dad we wouldn't have been able to budge it. We got it on the snow, my dad gave the cord a couple of pulls and it roared to life. He jumped on and took it for a little ride, then gave my sisters and me short rides. Then came the moment I had been waiting for; my turn to drive. With my dad on the back giving instructions I took over. Being in control of my first machine is a feeling I will never forget. I felt powerful in control of a large machine that could travel over the snow at high speed. I loved it. I could see many new possibilities for our war games. The SnoJet could be used as a specially designed tank used during winter combat operations in France. Guns blazing, my friends and I could now blast our way through enemy lines and free the prisoners of war.

The SnoJet did prove to be a regular source of winter fun and we kept it for years despite upgrading several times to new snowmobiles. And we did end up calling it "the tank" not so much because it played such an important role in our war games but because it seemed quite indestructible. In fact, to this day it sits on the side of my brother-in-law's garage. It probably still runs but the track finally tore off and it was impossible to get replacement parts from a company that went out of business in the mid-1970s. Although weeds grew up around and between the skis, it still looks good, which does not reflect its rough and tumble past. It rolled a number of times, like Chummy's jeep, down the mine's steep stock piles after failed climbing attempts.

My most enjoyable snowmobiling was with my friend Richie and involved traveling down long forgotten roads that could not be driven down in the summer. But in the winter, with the ground frozen and the absence of foliage, we could explore new territory and discover hidden meadows and sometimes abandoned homesteads. At one of the homesteads I found a kettle with its handle buried several inches into the flesh of an old maple tree. Someone had hung it on a small branch and never returned. Slowly, the tree grew around the handle so that the old rusty kettle was now part of the branch. We sat for awhile making up stories to explain how the kettle got left on the tree. This is not unlike what we archaeologists do today when we find an artifact of interest while excavating. We sit around thinking the behaviors that might have been responsible for putting this artifact in this location. All archaeologists in this situation dream of having a time machine that would enable us to dial up a date, like 1,000 BC, and travel back in time to see how close or how far off our interpretations might be.

A time machine is just what my dad and I seemed to be on one hot summer day when we were looking for raspberries. Raspberries often grow up around old homesteads and we traveled down a rarely used road just outside of Alpha coming to an old farm. My dad hadn't been back into the farm in over 20 years, ever since the man living there "went crazy" and was carted off to Newberry, the nearest state mental institution. No one had lived there since, and one of the out buildings had collapsed under the weight of a winter's snow. The weeds grew so high around the house that the first floor windows were hidden from view. My dad was right about the raspberries as they were so ripe and lush they fell off into your hand with only the slightest pressure. Both of our coffee cans were filled quickly despite the fact that I ate as many as I put in the container.

When the picking was done we walked up to the house as my dad told me the story of the man who had once lived there. He didn't know too much about him, only that his parents had died and his brothers and sisters had left long ago, leaving him with the farm. We peeked into the windows but the years of dust and grime made it difficult to see. My dad tried the door with a slight nudge and the rusted hinges squealed in protest. It wasn't surprising that it was unlocked as our own house in Alpha at the time didn't have door locks. He peered inside, gave me a mischievous smile and then motioned for me to follow him in, which I did with a mix of excitement and fear. We entered a formal front room that had an ornate sofa and chair next to a crank up phonograph. The floor and furniture were so covered in mice droppings and dust that our shoes made footprints as we crossed. There was a record on the phonograph and my dad gave the machine a few cranks, blew the dust off the record, and put down the needle and the record spun to life. When the needle hit the record it cracked with static but then filled the room with some ancient waltz. The sound made the hair on the back of my neck stand up and I was ready to bolt for the door but my dad laughed out loud and danced a little to the music. After listening to the haunting music for a minute or so, he turned off the phonograph and walked toward the kitchen. Certain that a skeleton was going to jump out at any moment, I followed anyway, holding onto the back of his shirt. A bowl, spoon, cup, and a box of cereal that had been tipped over and emptied long ago by ravaging mice, sat on the kitchen table. The men from the institution must have dragged him away while he was still eating breakfast. He didn't even get a chance to do his dishes or put away the cereal. We sat and stared for a minute or two, like Howard Carter and his assistant first peering into King Tut's tomb. You could almost see the guy sitting silently at the table, probably standing up, pushing the chair away and looking out the window as the state hospital car pulled into the yard. It suddenly become a sad place. We were looking at his last meal before being shipped off to the mental institution. Archaeology is sometimes like that. The joy of discovery can be overshadowed by the story that is unfolding when you find a child's burial or something else that brings someone's ancient sad story to life. We didn't touch anything else in the house and my dad finally said, "Let's go."

I visited the homestead years later while riding my dirt bike. Most of the windows were broken, the door was left open and the house had been picked clean. I suppose the family might have cleared some of it out but the locals did the rest. The joy, however, of exploring new areas on the snowmobile never left me. Richie and I found countless abandoned buildings and secret meadows accessible only in the winter. I loved being able to spin tales about the people who built these lost homesteads, and Richie liked the adventure of getting there, showing off his impressive back-country snowmobile riding that required busting a new path in deep snow instead of staying on the well groomed trails. My biggest snowmobile accident also happened with Richie right after we bought an Evinrude, which was two machines beyond the old SnoJet.

One afternoon after a long back-country race, Richie and I decided, sponta-neously, to race. After hours of maneuvering slowly through the woods we hit an old railroad grade, and it felt good to pick up speed on the well groomed trail. The trail split, one continuing on the railroad grade and the other going down a road that ran parallel to the tracks. Richie took the road but our race was no con-test as my path down the railroad grade was straight and flat while the road was full of twist and turns. Richie was an expert driver, and like a skilled horseman he navigated through the much more difficult course at a high speed, bouncing and swerving dangerously as he tried to stay up with me on the even, straight path. The railroad grade and the road merged left onto a larger road and I arrived first, and with my arm raised in victory I came to a stop. Richie was taking the race all the way back to town. He crashed into the back of my snowmobile and I raised my right foot in the air just in time as it would have been crushed by the front end of his Skidoo. Richie flew over the hood of the snowmobile but got up laugh-ing until he saw the damage done to our snowmobiles. His front bumper saved his machine from severe damage but there was still a puncture wound in the hood of his Skidoo. My taillight was smashed beyond recognition and the metal bar on the back was contorted and twisted out of shape.

Both snowmobiles ran OK but the trip back to town was slow because both of us dreaded having to show our fathers the damage. I, however, was dreading the confrontation less than Richie, which certainly would have surprised my friends. All of my friends were a bit afraid of my dad, which seemed odd to me. My image of him was a big cuddly bear, and I think they only saw the bear. I had to coax friends to come over when he was home. After they were around him for a while their fears might subside a little as he would always mess around with us playfully. Richie would have been surprised by my dad's reaction if he would have stayed around to see it. After I told Dad my story he simply said, "Seems like you were a little reckless. You and I are going to have to figure out a way to fix this before you can ride again." This was always my dad's way. He was never much for talking and he believed in action-oriented learning and discipline.

When I was about to turn 16, I mentioned that I wanted a pickup truck. I was shocked when he immediately said, "That would be a good idea." I soon learned that the pickup we had in mind was drastically different. He pulled into the driveway with a 1956 Dodge pickup with a flathead six, whose odometer had stopped just before it reach 160,000 miles. It barely ran. I was hoping for some-thing about 15 years newer, red, and a four-wheel drive. But it didn't take me long to warm up to his idea.

When he turned off the key, the engine refused to quit and he had to put it into gear to make it stop. Blueish smoke created a halo around the truck as he lowered his shoulder into the door to get it to open. The paint, a robin-egg blue, was peeling off in large sheets revealing a lime-green factory paint. It looked like someone had painted the truck with a brush as the streaks were still visible.

"If you want to own a vehicle you have to understand how they work," he said. As he came around the front of the truck he slammed his fist into the hood saying "They don't make them like this anymore."

I got to drive it just once before we had to put his plan into action.

"It needs new rings and bearings and YOU are going to do the work. What do you think of that?" he asked. I loved the idea.

I had heard the term "rings and bearings" many times but I really had no idea what they were.

"You're a smart kid, here's the book," is all he said as he handed me the repair manual for a 1956 flathead six Dodge.

I was given the entire two-car garage for the job and was excited to get started as I was inspired by my dad's confidence that I could actually do it. Before he left in the morning he would give me instructions and for the next two months he would stop home three to four times per day to check on my progress. My dad was not an experienced mechanic, but growing up on a farm forced him to figure out and fix things on his own. Over the years he had done similar overhauls.

"Remember you have to put this thing back together," he reminded me on the first day as I was simply piling the removed parts on a random heap. From that day foreword I lined up the parts in order of disassembly in neat rows. At night I would walk the rows, trying to recall each step and how the parts went back together.

Although it took me roughly 60 days to do the job a real mechanic could have done in two, one of the proudest moments of my life was hearing the truck roar to life. After seeing the entire truck laid out on the floor and putting every part back in, it was nothing short of miraculous to hear that engine start. My dad's head was under the hood when it started. He peered at the engine for awhile before pulling his head out, smiling and giving me a little wink. "Purrs like a kitten," is all he said.

He had a different style than most dads and a private family side that few people in Alpha would have expected. If they saw him watch a political speech I'm sure that they might change their minds entirely. The only time I ever saw my dad's tears was during a good speech by a Democrat. Speeches by Lyndon Johnson or Hubert Humphrey reduced him to mush. He would get so involved in it that he didn't realize that we were watching him. When he finally noticed he would look embarrassed for a second before grabbing one of us and giving us a tickle torture. Since this side of him was reserved for his family, his angry reputation persisted. In a small towns once you had a reputation, good or bad, it was almost impossible to change.

The town's people also tended to call on my dad when they needed someone responsible. Alpha always had a wonderful small-town 4th of July celebration, complete with a parade with kids dressed up in custumes, free ice-cream and cracker jacks, a nickel scramble, running races, and, of course, fireworks. The whole day was put on by our volunteer fire department, but by 9:00 p.m. most of the volunteers had too much to drink and were not permitted to shoot off the fireworks, so my dad was called into action. His fireman friend Bill was in charge of the fireworks and asked my dad each year to help him out as the rest of the fire crew could be counted on to start drinking by noon. He was the guy everyone could count on and there was no better example of this then the night Spokey, our neighbor, showed up at our door quite flustered. "It's my brother, he hasn't come back from the woods," Spokey stammered.

Spokey lived next door and his brother, Gerard, came to visit for extended periods, sometimes four months at a time. Their lot was as big as ours but it was entirely grown over with trees and bushes so that we couldn't even see his house. Every time Gerard came to visit he brought with him a new occupation and/or hobby for Spokey. The most obvious gift was the crates filled with pheasants. He had over two dozen pheasants in a large six-foot high pen, in an area larger than their house, that the two brothers had constructed one summer. During another visit, Gerard set up several bee hives on their property, leaving Spokey as bee keeper. Once when the queen left the hive it swarmed with the rest of the bees to our little choke cherry tree, which bent over from the weight. I got too close and the bees stung numerous times, punishing me for my curiosity. Spokey also raised beagles and always seemed to have puppies. Anytime I wanted he let me in the pen where I spent endless hours sitting in the middle of yipping puppies.

My dad had me run and get the flashlight and he and Spokey went off searching for Gerard who, we found out later, was trying to shoot a deer out of season ("violate") from a tree stand he had built. Gerard was always extremely thin and sickly looking and, according to town rumor, all of his internal organs were on the opposite side of his body. My dad and Spokey found Gerard dead at the base of a tree, which was a large maple that usually played some role in our summertime war games. He apparently fell out of the tree while waiting for a deer to come out to feed just before dark. I saw my dad and Spokey coming out of the woods, my dad holding the gun. When the sheriff came my dad told him what happened but tried to convince him to leave out of the report the part about violating for deer.

After I heard what happened to Gerard I recalled playing out in the backyard earlier in the day and hearing a strange noise. I walked to the edge of the woods and listened for about 10 minutes until it stopped. I guessed it was a cat, as they are known for making strange, sometimes human-like noises. I told my dad what I had heard.

"What time was that?" my dad inquired.

"Just before dark," I answered. "Do you think it could have been Gerard calling for help after he fell out of the tree?" I wondered. I had never heard such a noise before but I had convinced myself at the time that it was a cat but now I was left to wonder if it could have been Gerard crying out weakly after he had fallen. "Maybe he was alive for a long time and I could have gotten help."

My dad considered his answer and after a short pause said, "Don't worry about it." And I didn't, even though it did seem likely that I was hearing Gerard's final painful calls for help.

My dad did not seem to care about what people thought about him, one way or the other, and he used his mean reputation to his great advantage whenever necessary. One day I looked out the window to find several older boys climbing on our fence, probably looking for some attention from my sisters. My sisters and I helped my dad build the fence the summer before. It was made out of cedar, which my dad cut from the swamp, and had two horizontal cedar poles between each post. We helped him peel the logs, pace off the distance between postholes, and we held the beams in place as he drove in the spikes. We even got to nail a few on but our arms would soon tire and he would have to take over.

I watched the older boys for a while from our window. My sisters weren't home but the boys didn't know that so they did their best to show off. They walked on the fence like they were acrobats on a high wire. This was no big deal. We had mastered this feat the same day the fence went up. They then played a game of chicken, trying to knock one another off the pole and fall to the ground with excessive drama meant for my sisters. One kid started to jump on the fence causing the pole to bend dangerously. Soon, all three of them climbed up and started to jump, balancing by hanging onto a nearby branch, and the pole bent farther than I thought possible. It was just a matter of time before it would break.

Unfortunately for them, my dad pulled up in the driveway just as they were reaching a new level of bouncing. His face crunched up into an angry scowl as he saw the boys on the fence, now bending ever closer to breaking. They were having so much fun that they didn't see him until he slammed the door and took a step toward them. They froze. My dad yelled so loud that I could hear what he said from inside the house.

"Hey, what the hell do you think you are doing?" He said it in a voice that I only rarely heard; lower than his normal voice and with a touch of a snake's hiss. I'd seen these boys sass back at teachers and our principal many times so I braced myself for a confrontation. Instead, they took off like they had seen a ghost. One of the boys slipped off the still bouncing beam and came down hard on his arm.

He jumped up quickly but I could see he was holding his arm as the three of them, tripping and falling over one another, ran out of the yard.

Most boys think of their dads, at least for a short time during their lives, as a bigger than life super hero. Although my dad, like anyone else, had his faults, I tend to think he gave me more reasons than most dads for me to idolize him as a real life action figure. There was no greater evidence of this than the times he crashed through doors, just like I'd seen on TV. I was there for both door shattering feats but personally recall just one. It was early summer and we were near Houghton, probably to pick strawberries in the nearby fields. For a special treat we stopped for lunch in the newly opened Kentucky Fried Chicken. It was a treat because there were few chain restaurants in the U.P., so we always felt a little deprived when we saw ads for McDonalds or KFC. After our enjoyable feast on the Colonels secret recipe, my mother excused herself to go to the bathroom, not far from our table. After a few minutes we heard the door rattle and then shake as my mother had locked the door and now could not get out. She started to panic as she was a little claustrophobic. We heard a faint, "Matt," from the bathroom and then a more frantic scream, "Matt!" My dad got up immediately, tried to open the door unsuccessfully then briefly tried to talk my mom out of the room but she was too frantic at this point to listen. His jaw clenched and his eyebrows furrowed into a mean glare. "Stand back," he said to her and loud enough so that now everyone in the restaurant turned their attention to the scene. My dad took one step back, lowered his right shoulder slightly, and then with one powerful thrust broke open the door. With the frame of the door in splinters he reached in, grabbed my mother by the hand and just said, "Let's go kids." I remember walking out of the KFC and everyone, including the workers, stood by in silent disbelief. When we were back in the car I really wanted to talk about the event but it took maybe 30 miles or so before my mom had recovered from the trauma of being locked in. Finally, one of my sisters said, "I can't believe you broke the door down," making us all erupt in laughter.

The other door breaking incident occurred when I was an infant. My mother put me down for a nap on their bed and closed the door so I wouldn't be disturbed by my playful, noisy sisters. Unfortunately, the door locked when she closed it but she didn't discover this until sometime later when she tried to get in and check on me. She became frantic and called my father at work who raced home in only 15 minutes. By the time he got home I was crying quite hysterically, according to my mother who might have been transferring her fear of being locked in a room. Without saying a word, or breaking stride, my dad stormed into the house and crashed through the door. A several inch wide strip of the frame door broke away, which he never did fix. I suspect that he found it best that our family stay away from locking doors.

My dad also took his work seriously, which is another reason for his tough reputation. Whether he was on the job, mowing the lawn, raking leaves, or working in the garden, my dad attacked his work and wore the scowl of a prize fighter while doing it. This was the image most people had of my dad as they drove or walked past our house or saw him at his job. If they knew him better they knew that his tempered flared rarely and if it did it was usually when he confronted an obstacle while doing some task. A board refusing to bend into shape would trigger a fierce vein bulging effort to make it right. If he hit a rock when digging a hole, he would take it as a personal insult. Either the rock or the shovel was going to give way in a flurry of sweat and blood. Every time he worked he cut his finger or hand, which had become one big mass of scar tissue. Forcing a screw, yanking at a stubborn root, or pushing on a pry bar would inevitably lead to a wound, which he never attended to until the job was done. All of our jobs were baptized in his blood.

As an enthusiastic home project do-it-yourselfer, I seem to have inherited my father's propensity for injury. Although I don't cut myself with the frequency or severity that my dad did, it brings on a strange sense of self-reflective joy when I do. It is probably a little odd to get a warm and fuzzy feeling while watching yourself bleed, as long as the wound is not too severe. Most people probably get a similar feeling when they pull an old teddy bear out of a box, while I sit down and smile watching blood ooze out of a wound.

Growing up I got accustomed to seeing blood running down his hand or dripping on the board, or so I thought. One job that I particularly disliked was cutting large pieces of wood with our underpowered table saw. I hated those big cutting jobs because my task was always to hold the ends of the two cut boards as he fed it through the saw. If I held it too high or too low or too far to the left or right, the blade would bind and come to a stop. My dad would motion with his head the direction he wanted me to move or lift the board, which only sometimes worked. I never understood why the blade really got stuck, it seemed like a random event as I did my best to hold the boards straight and true. The ultimate reason could have been that I wasn't strong enough to hold the boards properly during the last stage of cutting when I had most of the weight.

I was eating my favorite breakfast, toast with peanut butter and banana slices, dreaming about going for a ride on the SnoJet when my dad pulled up with several pieces of plywood sticking out of the back of his pickup. I moaned. He walked up the back steps into our kitchen and poked his head in the door.

"Give me a hand when you're done," he said, which really meant he wanted my help now, so I pulled on my coat and followed him outside jamming the rest of my peanut butter and banana on toast in my mouth. These were massive pieces of plywood but my dad could lift them by himself so my only job was to open doors and move things out of the way as he made it down the stairs into the basement. We laid out the plywood, he measured and drew out a line, and he switched on the saw as he wrestled the big piece of plywood into place. I got into my position, ready to catch the boards.

"Hold them even," my dad reminded me above the whine of the saw tearing into the boards. When the cut was about half done we started to run into problems. The plywood was so big and the saw so small that all I could see was the blade above the board, which kept binding and moaning to a stop. Despite our best efforts, the problems got worse and the cutting progressed by little spurts of the blade as it temporarily spun free. The blade was now stopping more than spinning and the electric motor started to make funny sounds. I could sense my dad's frustration as he jerked the board, swore, jerked the board and swore again. He moved to the side of the saw and gave the board a fateful jerk that sent his hand into the blade as it spun free. Blood and grizzle flew off the blade and made a straight line down the board almost making it all the way to me. He grabbed his hand and inspected it quickly. I dropped my end of the board and the saw's motor moaned on the verge of burning out. The board bent and started to crack. He reached under the board and cut the power, then covered the cut on his finger with his other hand and yelled, "The board is breaking, pick up your end," which I did immediately and with renewed strength. He grabbed an old rag and wrapped his finger tightly and bounded up the stairs three at a time. I stood there struggling with the load wondering if he had cut the finger all the way off and, more importantly, if it was my fault. Feeling a little queasy, I stared at the line of blood and grizzle and noticed that it did not match the pencil line, which may have explained our problems with the stuck blade.

Several agonizing minutes later he was back with a hastily made bulky wrapping on his little finger, and he looked at me, my arms quivering from the load. He picked up my end of the board and said, "Good job holding up the board, it was starting to break." After a short rest he said, "Ready to try again?" I nodded my head. He fired up the saw and we finished the cut without incident, this time following the blood instead of the pencil line.

My mom, dad and I were watching Walter Cronkite that night and my dad kept moving his cut hand trying to get it comfortable. My mom had replaced the makeshift bandage after applying a healthy dose of hydrogen peroxide. During the news my sisters were occasionally absent because they were upstairs listening to records, such as *Hey Jude* by the Beatles, the top song of 1968. Like a lot of parents during that era, they didn't like rock-n-roll and they wondered, along with many of their friends, whether pop music was one of the reasons why the country seemed to be going to the pits. Nonetheless, they let my sisters buy the latest music with the stipulation that they play it upstairs. This really wasn't much help, however, because you could still hear every word of each song in our living room. When the music would start, my father would glance up at the ceiling and the crack he patched just several weeks earlier. My sisters turned their upstairs bedroom into an American Bandstand stage and they played each record over and over until they knew every single word. Once the words were memorized they would start dancing and often invite their friends over to listen and dance. The action got so intense during one summer that a crack developed in the ceiling of our living room right below their dance floor. When Mary Fran, Karen and their friends were all up there dancing it sounded like "charging buffalo," so my dad showed them the crack and told them to hold down the crazy dancing. He patched it but every time the music started he would glance up waiting for the crack to appear once again.

My sisters' bedroom was a converted attic and the only room on the second floor of our house. It was a wonderful sanctuary and I snuck up there when they weren't around. The walls were paneled but painted a nice "girl" color and the ceiling was angled at the corners following the roof line, which forced my dad to walk with his head bent over when he came up. The long, skinny room had a built in desk and dresser drawers, and there was a window at each end. The north window looked into the woods and the south window gave the best view, summer or winter, of Bear Cave Hill. This would also be the perfect place for a machine gunner, should the enemy attack up the hill.

Each side of their room had small doors without knobs, which concealed the entryway into attics and added to their mystery. The walkway past the stairs was so narrow that a knob would have gotten in the way so the door was opened by putting your fingers in the gap at the bottom and tugging, releasing a magnetic catch.

Going through the doors was like entering a another world. In their bedroom it was bright, colorful, and fresh, but once through the doors it was a dark and musty room where the air was thick and stale. This adventure was usually done in the spring or fall for in the summer the attic heat was unbearable and in the winter the attic was filled with arctic air too cold for exploration. A pull on the string turned on the solitary light bulb that illuminated a museum full of old treasures.

The room was dominated by hanging clothes, which made it difficult to navigate, and as you got farther from the door and the only light, it not only got darker but the floor became hazardous. There were nailed down boards near the attic door but as you went back into the attic you walked hunched over on ever more precarious boards, eventually balancing on a single plank. At the front of the attic were things I recognized; dresses my mom wore last year, my dad's old bowling ball, and boxes of my cousins handed down clothes that I would one day grow into. I loved to explore the attic. Each time I opened the door it was like cracking open and peeking into an Egyptian tomb. I would crawl around sneaking a look inside boxes searching for treasures from ancient times.

During one attic visit my exploration was rewarded. I pried open an old box and discovered a handmade slingshot formed from Y-shaped tree branch. The bark was removed and the ridges and bumps were whittled smooth with great care. The sling was made of rubber from an old inner tube and there was a small leather pouch to hold a rock. I took the sling shot out of the attic to inspect it in better light. I held it up, pulled back the rubber and gave it a test. It seemed like the rubber still had lots of power despite sitting in the attic for an unknown amount of time.

I carried the new find down the stairs and found my mother in the kitchen. "Mom, what is this?" I asked. I handed it to her and she inspected it with a puzzled look on her face. As she turned it over in her hand her look was replaced with recognition and a smile. "Your father made this a long time ago when you were just a baby, really. He spent a whole afternoon on it. But you were way too young for such a thing so we put it away and forgot about it."

"Can I have it now?" I asked hopefully.

"Sure, why not. Just be careful. Don't shoot at anybody or near the house."

I spent many hours perfecting my sling shot skill. It didn't shoot as far or hard as other kid's store-bought wrist rockets, but I would not have traded it for anything. When I wasn't shooting it, I had it in my back pocket always ready if a bird or chipmunk should come into range. I practiced nonstop. First I could hit a tree, then I could at least make a bird fly or chipmunk jump by coming close. I hit a robin once, but it flew away unhurt.

Finding that slingshot in the attic prompted countless return trips. I discovered that as you went farther from the attic door you went back in time. There were old dresses, out-of-date sport jackets, and hat boxes that had not moved once since I could remember. It was a bit spooky but the journey was worth it because all the way to the back was my all-time favorite find: my dad's full dress military uniform. It hung so far in the back that the single light bulb near the door only served as a beacon for my return and provided no illumination. This trip was best done on a sunny day because some light came in the ventilation grate on the back wall. But even in the weak light provided by the beams of sun coming from the slats, the uniform still looked proud and new. His cap was in a bag on a nearby hook. I always put the jacket and hat on and practiced my salute. Because of the low ceiling I had to be on my knees so the coat dragged on the floor. I always carefully brushed off the dust each time I hung it back up. It looked so powerful hanging there and I imagined how my dad must have looked with it on. I wanted to be a soldier just like him. I wanted to fight with other brave men for our country. I wanted to win battles, save lives, and become a hero, just like my dad. I smelled his coat. It had the musty smell of the attic but other unfamiliar smells as well.

I carried the coat and hat out of the attic and put it on and stood at attention as I stared out the window. Bear Cave Hill stared back at me. From this distance it was just a white gash in the brown hillside. I scowled at the hill feeling strong and courageous. "I am going to conquer you!" I yelled out the window. "I'm going to ride you!"

Chapter 9

Bear Cave Hill

The clock said 3:57 a.m. but I was wide awake. It was Christmas morning and the excitement of new toys and games woke me up from a sound sleep. My list was a little longer than usual but my parents seemed to be in a buying mood lately. I decided to get up and take a peek, but it was so warm in my bed that I hesitated because I was not anxious to pull the covers off and introduce the cool night air to the warmth of my cocoon. I decided to wait for the furnace to come on, which would provide a warm blast of air and make the transition much easier. I wouldn't have to wait long because it was a clear, cold night and the furnace was on more than off. Through my window I could see the near full moon and the twinkle of distant stars. The reflection of the moonlight off the snow provided so much light that it really didn't seem like night at all. It had been warm enough on Christmas Eve for some of the snow to melt on the trees and bushes, forming tiny icicles on each branch. The moon's reflection made each bush and tree twinkle like stars as they moved in the gentle breeze. Yesterday was spent at the my grandparents house, exchanging family gifts and gorging ourselves with food. Today would be a day for just our family, opening gifts from "Santa Claus" and going to church.

The furnace roared to life and in seconds it was blasting warm dry air so I decided to take a peek at my booty under the tree. My new pajamas, opened last night, hung on my body awkwardly as the creases from the packaging still had not flattened out. We got new pajamas for "Christmas morning pictures," but I would have preferred to wear my old ones, which were soft, the waste band was stretched out for additional comfort, and they smelled good. Wearing the new ones was like hugging a stranger.

To get to the living room and the tree, I had to pass right by the open door of my parent's bedroom. They both slept lightly and if they woke up I knew they would force me to lie in bed for at least another unbearable hour. A couple of years ago if I woke up at this time I would just start yelling and jumping on their bed and I would run upstairs to rouse my sisters. They should have been grateful that I just wanted to take a peek at the presents without disturbing anyone. I walked gingerly out my door and began the daring trip past their room. During the day I never heard the floor squeak but during this quiet night the floor protested with a squeak or a pop with each step. Our old house made lots of noises at night so my goal was to walk slow enough so that each creak and groan from the floor was so widely separated in time that their unconscious would not be alerted. This required the patience of a cat sneaking up on a mouse. By the time I was right in front of their door, which hadn't closed properly since I was an infant, the furnace stopped blowing reducing some of my background cover noise. Now I could hear my parents breathing restfully, but each time my step made a loud enough noise their gentle breath patterns would be interrupted with a groan or snort.

I made it safely down the hall onto the quieter carpeting in front of the tree. The light from the moon and the single street lamp on the corner provided enough light to see. The bottom of the tree was overflowing with gifts, placed so nicely under the tree that it seemed as if they emerged from the tree itself. It was so beautiful and so quiet. Soon the peace would be broken by a flurry of unwrapping and the blaze of my dad's Bell and Howell camera fitted with the row of blinding spot lights. I liked it better at night like this. I laid down in front of the tree, which twinkled in the dim light like the outside bushes and trees.

The twinkle on our tree, however, was created by thousands of strings of shimmery silver tinsel. All Polish families used a lot of tinsel but nobody put more on than my family. We could put up the tree and string the lights and hang the bulbs in about 20 minutes, but the ritual placing of the tinsel would take the rest of the afternoon and sometimes into the next day. We saved last year's tinsel in the pages of old Sears and Roebuck catalogs, to keep the strands flat and wrinkle free. A few new packages were opened each year but most of it came from the pile of catalogs carefully stored in our basement.

I must have dozed off in front of the tree because the next thing I knew it was light outside and I found myself curled up in the fetal position trying to keep warm, uncovered on the cool floor. The sound of my sisters pounding down their bedroom stairs woke me and I sat up just as they burst into the room. During the next few minutes we were like sharks in a feeding frenzy, all captured for eternity in the blaze of the Bell and Howell. The pace slowed as we opened gifts from each other. I loved to watch my sisters open gifts from me. I put a lot of thought into the gift, and as they opened it my skin would get warm and my stomach would tickle with butterflies. They always smiled and said they loved it. I loved it more.

Soon after opening gifts we dressed for church, which was crowded with visiting families. The excitement of Christmas morning and the blotches of light in our eyes from the blinding lights of my dad's movie camera made it hard to concentrate in church. Our small church was filled to over-capacity and my dad helped to set up folding chairs in the aisles. We were dressed in our Sunday best but no one knew because winter coats were kept on and buttoned up. The furnace was turned up just 20 minutes before Mass but it wasn't enough to get the chill out. The seats were still cold to the touch. No one complained because if the furnace was turned up too much the priest would not have enough money to pay the fuel bill and he would have to ask the congregation for help. No one liked a homily that asked for money. But after such a request, the next week's bulletin would always thank the congregation for the anonymous check to cover the overdue bill. We always guessed the donor was Mrs. Mottes, the neatly dressed old widow who always sat in the back pew.

Her husband died in a mine accident before WWII and when their only child was very young. For several decades thereafter right up until the early 1960s Mrs Mottes was the post mistress, a well-paying and coveted job. Except for the school teachers, she was the only female salaried employee in Alpha at that time. I often wonder who was responsible for the singular act of kindness that made Mrs. Mottes the post mistress soon after she was widowed and no doubt headed for a difficult and uncertain future. The history of Alpha and most small towns is made up countless acts of kindness as the town's people struggled to survive in difficult times. Our church and the people of Alpha were ultimately the beneficiaries as Mrs. Mottes saved wisely and then was able to generously share her accumulated wealth.

We had a small but enthusiastic congregation. They met for years in the village hall or any available space before we were assigned a pastor who directed the construction of the church. You would never know by looking at it, but St. Edwards was built from an enormous building that the mining company donated. It was moved into place with volunteer labor and transformed into a church by the local men in two to three hour spurts after their shift at the mine was over. Local families donated money for the stained glass and soon an old mine building looked like a church.

No one really knew what do to on Christmas afternoon. Most of the time we just laid around like gorged lions after a big kill. I was sitting on the edge of our L-shaped sofa and my dad was on the other end watching Karen play one of her new games while I watched him. Years later we would sit in similar spots watching my wife and two kids on the floor playing a game. I looked up and my dad was looking at me. This would be our last holiday together as the doctors gave him just a couple of months to live. I saw the x-rays. Even a lay person like me could see that things weren't right. Both lungs had cancer and it had traveled into the bones of his shoulder.

"There's going to be a lot of pain," the doctor told us. In character, dad never complained but as he napped his true feelings would come out as he would moan from the pain in his sleep. At this point he was able to take morphine whenever he wanted. When he took the max he was comfortable but would doze off.

From the father a son learns to be a man. A father defines manhood but it has taken me a lifetime to completely understand my father's lessons. Manhood is not about winning on the battlefield or conquering one's fears but rather it's about brotherhood. To become a man you must find someone you are willing to die for and also have someone who loves you enough to die for you whether it is in an iron mine, on a football field, in battle, or just in your house. These trials of courage, endurance, and strength test our manhood, but it is the bonds of brotherhood that create it. I learned my first lesson of manhood on Bear Cave Hill.

On Christmas afternoon in 1968, I glanced outside toward our sledding hill and Joey was there by himself. I dressed and joined him on the hill. It was a cold, sunny, bright day; the kind of day that gave you a headache from squinting. We took a few runs but it wasn't as much fun with just two people. My eyes settled on Bear Cave Hill and I blurted out these fateful words, "Want to go down Bear Cave Hill?" Joey's head snapped over to look at the hill, then he slowly turned his head toward me.

"Yeah, let's do it," he said with a wicked smile on his face. A cold chill ran through my blood and I could feel my heart start to race with both fear and excitement.

"Our toboggan is busted," I said. "We broke off the front of it trying to pull too many kids behind the snowmobile." We both thought about our predicament for a second when I said, "But we could go down on our big inner tube."

Besides providing countless hours of bouncing and rolling fun, inner tubes were the fastest things on snow. But they were also uncontrollable. Sleds and toboggans could be steered somewhat or at least you could be assured that they would go in a straight line but inner tubes seemed to have a mind of their own when going down a hill. Each time down the hill was an adventure as half the time you would be traveling backwards, and when it hit a bump a new course would be charted.

"Nobody has ever gone down Bear Cave in an inner tube," Joey said with the excitement of a new feat, which he no doubt felt matched his sense of adventure and dare. "Plus they're great in deep snow." I would have been satisfied going down the old fashioned way, on a wooden toboggan, but without any better options I walked home and grabbed the inner tube resting against a tree near the edge of our yard.

Joey and I tested the tube together on our sledding hill. There was enough room for both of us to lie down on our stomachs but there was little to hang onto. The best way was for each of us to put an arm around each other and use our free arm to wrap around the outside edge of the tube for at least some support. Together we successfully made it down our sledding hill but the crown on the road kept us against the snowbank the entire trip and we spun around like a ride at the carnival. This seemed like a dangerous way to get down Bear Cave Hill, which was only 10 feet wide or so without snow banks, but before I could express my hesitancy Joey said, "This things perfect."

To get there we walked right down the middle of the main road coming into town. Traffic on the busiest days meant a car every minute or so, on Christmas Day hardly anyone was on the road and not a single car passed us by. We walked past the frozen creek and we slid a little on an exposed patch of ice. We got down on our hands and knees and could see the occasional fish beneath the clear ice. Once we were over the creek it was time to walk the half mile or so cross-country in the deep snow. We took turns pulling the tube and we jumped on it anytime there was even a small hill. The deep snow kept our progress very slow but not a word was said about our goal. Like warriors marching into battle we avoided the subject yet we talked almost nonstop. We shared the most recent knock-knock jokes and when they ran out we got to one of our favorite topics, listing all the words we knew for pecker. We played this so many times that I could rattle off a half dozen without hardly moving my lips. "Cock, dick, pecker, pee-pee, ding-dong, and *moochacha*."

"*Moochacha*" was the Polish slang word for pecker and it was one of the first words that I remember learning. My mother or sisters would be zipping up my pants, pajamas, or snow pants and my dad would yelp, "Watch out for his '*moochacha*!'" Then he would smile and wink at me and then do a mock scowl at the women, sometimes wagging his finger. This was an important early lesson; the *moochacha* is very important and requires a great deal of attention and care and women need to be constantly reminded of this.

After we had thought we had exhausted the list of words for *moochacha* we could always come up with some more. When we put our minds to it there was really and endless number of less specific words and we took turns coming up with them to pass the time.

"Thing."

"It"

"Friend."

"Little buddy."

"Little Elvis."

Each one of these was followed by giggling, and we would laugh even more after exploring the many ways each of these words could be used in a sentence.

My stomach muscles ached from the combination of pulling the tube, walking in deep snow, and laughing, which made me less aware of the butterflies that were churning in my gut. I was scared. Joey probably was too, but he sure didn't show it. I hoped that I didn't show it either.

We finally made it to the base of the ski jump landing. The recent snow had covered up any trace of previous use earlier in the winter. I was happy to see that the soft, billowy snow made the jump and landing seem less intimidating. We took a break at the base of the hill and rested before starting the climb. Today, Christmas day 1968, we would be tested and we would become men. We both glanced over at the toboggan graveyard, but the evidence of the former rides and crashes were buried beneath the blanket of snow, the winter swallowing up their stories. We then craned our necks almost straight up and looked up the hill, and at that moment a bead of sweat traveled straight down my spine, followed by a violent shiver. I looked over at Joey and he was smiling and we seemed to be thinking the same thing, "Let's kick its ass!"

Our enthusiasm gave us a burst of energy and we started charging up the hill. But our ascent was soon slowed by the steep and slippery grade. With each step a small avalanche of snow would cascade down the hill. Progress was best made on hands and knees and we took turns pulling and pushing the tube, careful not to let it go. Occasionally, we would lie down on our backs to rest and let our hearts slow down. By the time we got half way up, I was so tired that I wasn't afraid anymore; I just wanted to get to the top and get it over with.

With Joey pulling and me pushing the tube, we finally neared the top and the steepest part of the hill. I was looking forward to getting to the top and resting, but just as we reached the highest point Joey jumped on and the tube finally was permitted to do what it had been yearning for the entire climb. As the tube passed I jumped on, half on Joey, half on the tube. We rocketed downward faster than I had ever traveled on snow, the rush of air feeling icy cold on my sweaty face. We stayed remarkably straight going down the hill until about half way when we started to rotate slowly counter clockwise so that we were traveling sideways as we approached the jump. The rotation must have put us off course slightly because when I craned my neck for a look down hill, we were about to go off the side of the jump. Joey had a better view as he was on the downhill side of our quarter-turned tube. This position also made him more vulnerable to injury as we barreled off the side of the jump. We missed the biggest part of the liftoff but we were still airborne. The angle of the jump actually caused the tube to tilt up putting us almost in a standing position as we flew toward the trees side by side—my left hand still clinging to the tube and my right wrapped tightly around Joey's waist. Arm-in-arm we hit a tree, a small one that gave way but did little to slow our progress as we headed further off course toward the bigger trees. That's the last thing I remember.

I am unsure how long we laid unconscious in the snow. The first thing I remember was my own breathing; heavy, slow nighttime breathing with long inhalations, a slight pause and then the exhalation through my nose and mouth. I heard and felt myself breathing like I was blowing into a microphone placed in a large, empty, dark hall. I had no other sensation, only inky blackness. Breathe in, breathe out, like soft whispering pines. Then pain. Pain, like a sword through my eye, woke me out of this sleep. I scrunched up my face and struggled to open my eyes that felt like they had elephants standing on the lids. When I finally forced them open I saw that the day was no longer bright and sunny as clouds had covered the sun and a light snow had started to fall. I raised my head and realized that we had traveled well into the woods. I had a hard time focusing because my right eye was completely blurred. I pushed myself up and turned my head downhill and found Joey beside me resting against a large maple tree, which was to blame for our final stop. He was face down in the snow so I rolled him over toward me.

"Joey!" I yelled. His eyes were shut and he didn't seem to be breathing. I felt nauseous and it wouldn't have taken much to make me barf. I thought he was dead. His hat was tipped sideways as it always was after a big wipe out. I grabbed him by the coat and shook him but still he didn't move. I didn't know what to do. I started to cry. I don't ever remember crying like this. It started without warning and the usual slow buildup when you had a chance to fight it back. I continued to shake Joey and shout his name between hysterical sobs. It was my idea to take the tube. It was my fault. My cries and sobs were swallowed up by the woods and the lightly falling snow. I looked away and gazed around trying to collect myself and figure out what to do. I couldn't leave Joey and get help and I wouldn't be able to drag him out.

A sick groan shifted my attention back to Joey. He was alive! Eyes still closed, he moved his jaw up and down like he was chewing on something sticky, and he brought his hand up to his head. "Joey!" I screamed. "Joey are you OK?" He opened his eyes but didn't seem to focus well. "You OK?" I asked again. He still didn't reply, but raised himself to sitting with a grimace of pain. He looked around and seemed to remember what we had done.

"Jeez," is all he said. He looked back at me. If he could tell I had been crying he didn't let on. "Jeez," he said again.

"You OK?" I asked yet again.

"My head hurts," he said as he started to stand. He was so caught up in his own pain that I don't think he noticed my involuntary post-crying hicks.

"Can you walk?" I asked. He limped a little as he took a couple of steps.

"I think so." You OK?"

"I'm OK" I said and noticed again that one half of my field of vision was blurred. "You want to try to walk back?"

Joey nodded his head. "Where is the tube?" We looked around and saw the trail it took down the hill bouncing off trees as it went. We followed the trail and found the tube at the bottom of the hill resting peacefully no worse for the wear and certainly unaware of the feat it had just played a role in.

We walked home slowly. Joey hobbled along looking at the ground as we walked without saying a word. I found it easier to keep my blurred right eye closed when walking. The trip seemed to take forever. I was aware of each step I took and I had to will each leg to go on. I walked Joey to his doorstep. He looked back at me when he opened the door but we parted without a word as the traumatic ride still filled our minds. I walked up to my house dragging the tube behind.

Through the window I could see my mom working at the sink. I walked into the porch, took off my boots and opened the kitchen door.

"What happened?" my mother gasped as she came toward me with a concerned look on her face. I didn't realize that I looked noticeably bad. Before I could answer she was pawing over me like a mother dog licking her puppy that had been lost. "Matt, look at this!" she said as her hands investigated my head and face. My dad was peeling potatoes at the kitchen table, his nightly ritual. He could peel enough potatoes for the whole family in a couple of minutes, and the blade moved so fast that I couldn't follow it. He could also peel an entire apple in one long, thin, peel. His peeling slowed down to a human pace as he watched my mom take off my jacket and start to feel my shoulders, elbows, arms, and fingers. "Let's see your teeth?" she said sternly. I opened my mouth and she inspected them quickly, saw no damage and moved her investigation to my back and legs.

I noticed that my vision was not blurred anymore because, apparently, my right eye was now swollen shut. I touched it with my fingers. It didn't feel like mine.

"Where do you hurt?" she asked as she inspected my eye.

"Mostly my head," I said meekly. I had the worst headache of my life.

"Now tell me what happened?" my mother said as she sat down in the chair ready to listen after she was convinced nothing was broken. She wanted some of the details before pulling out the peroxide.

I paused, my mother raised her eyebrows in anticipation and my dad stopped peeling altogether. "Nothing, really," I lied. "Joey and I were sledding. We took a nasty wipe out."

But it was so much more than that, I thought to myself. I had been sure that Joey was dead and that it was my fault. I doubted that I could really explain it. The image of him lying in the snow, motionless, came racing back in my mind. The pain of that image overwhelmed the pain of my smashed head and bruised body.

"How is Joey?" my mom asked.

"OK, I guess," I said unconvincingly. I decided to tell more of the story. I swallowed hard. "Joey and I wiped out. Joey really hit his head. He was knocked out for a little bit. I thought he was….dead." When I said the word "dead" my voice cracked and one of my involuntary post-crying hicks made my whole head spasm.

"Well, my goodness, he's not dead," my mother said sounding a bit perplexed.

I looked up and saw my dad. His eyes were filled with tears as were mine. Through our misty eyed vision I saw right into his soul. I saw the pain of brothers left behind and the guilt of thinking there might have been more he could have done. He put his enormous hand on mine, gave me a sad smile and nodded his head slightly. He then winked at me, nodded his head again, picked up his potato and knife and went back to peeling. My mother, usually much more perceptive about such things, didn't understand the fear and guilt brought about by the event. But my father did.

This moment has become more important through the years and it was especially meaningful on the day of my own father's death.

There were several days between when my dad died and his funeral. At first there was lots to take care of, make the funeral arrangements, write his obituary, and greet well-wishers, but soon there got to be long periods without anything to do in my parent's crammed house. It was spring so we went for walks around their 40 acres, where my dad and I had spent so many hours working together and they had now built a house. My brother-in-law noticed a porcupine on top of a large maple tree near the back of the property. Porcupines are a menace as they can kill a whole patch of trees in no time. We mentioned it to my mom, and she said, "If your dad were here he would shoot it."

There was no doubt about that. Some people called him the "Section 6 Assassin" as he wasn't afraid to exterminate, as a last resort, any of the wildlife that would feed upon their precious trees, shrubs, vegetable garden, and flowers that they had worked so hard to cultivate.

"I'll get it," I said hesitantly. I hadn't shot a gun in 15 years, so I enlisted the help of my brother-in-law, Bob, and his son, Marc, who were experienced hunters. I grabbed a single-shot 20 gauge shotgun and a couple shells and Marc picked up the more powerful 12 gauge for backup. It was about a quarter mile walk to the tree, but we could see the porcupine clearly as soon as we rounded the corner of the house. Hidden by the foliage for much of the year, the animal stood out clearly against the sky as the trees had just started to bud out. We walked near the base of the tree but the porcupine continued eating quite confidently perched so high in the tree and well armored with a blanket of quills. Evolution moves too slowly for them to learn to fear men with guns. Bob and Marc looked at me and I said, "I'll do it." Part of me didn't want to kill this creature, but another part needed to do it, not because I needed to kill something to make my grief go away but instead because my mom wanted it done and he wasn't there for her. Being a man, I had learned, is also about doing things, without complaint, that might be difficult.

I cracked the single-shot gun and loaded a shell. This was a long shot for a relatively small gauge gun so I worried that I would miss. Marc loaded the 12 gauge just in case. I took comfort in the fact that I was once a good shot. As I pulled back the hammer and took aim, it all seemed quite familiar. I took a deep breath, squeezed the trigger and the 20 gauge erupted. The porcupine was motionless for a second and then let go of the branch and fell to the ground with a thud. It started to get up and walk and Marc finished it off with the 12 gauge. My dad would have been proud, not because we killed something but because we did what had to be done.

*   *   *

I often stand on the dock of the historic Farrell Cottage where my field crew and I stay while we work on Grand Island, just off the southern shore of Michigan's Upper Peninsula. I've been working here since my father died; digging into the U.P.'s history from 1000 BC until the very recent past, a 20th century logging camp. Dad worked in a camp much like the one we are investigating and it feels right to peer into this time period.

The dock is a favorite place of mine on the island. It is built with two rock cribs designed to withstand the tortures of the Lake Superior ice, but lately the lake has been winning the battle as the dock has bowed dramatically making it difficult to keep your footing at night. But night is when I seek out the dock. On cloudless nights the stars seem to come down around me as their images reflect in the lake. The waves come in slowly at times and lap gently against the eight foot sandstone beachhead, but at other times they roll in with such fury that I have to raise my voice to be heard by a person standing right next to me. On calm nights it is so quiet that I can unintentionally eavesdrop on conversations aboard sailboats moored across the bay. Once or twice per season I see the Northern Lights dancing just above the horizon or arcing across the entire sky in a dramatic display.

On clear nights I always look for the North Star, Polaris, which for centuries guided mariners and travelers. The Big Dipper and the rest of the cosmos twirl around the North Star as if tethered to it with a giant rope. I look to the North Star every chance I get because it has become a symbol of my father. If souls become stars, as they do in many legends, than my father's soul is the North Star—not flashy and brilliant, but unchanging, unmoving, easy to find, and quite functional. Late at night when I am sure that I am alone, I raise both of my arms to the star so that I become the spinning axis with a direct connection to the North Star. I then say a few words, not too many because words aren't our style. Mostly I just sit with him for a while.

978-0-595-37939-2
0-595-37939-7